IMAGES OF THE
SPANISH
CIVIL WAR

Above: Children making a Fascist salute before a poster of Franco.
Overleaf: Republican ideal of a militiaman, 1936.

IMAGES OF THE SPANISH CIVIL WAR

Introduction by Raymond Carr

GEORGE ALLEN & UNWIN

LONDON   SYDNEY

copyright © Allen & Unwin (Publishers) Ltd 1986
Introduction copyright © Raymond Carr 1986

Allen & Unwin (Publishers) Ltd
40 Museum Street, London WC1A 1LU, UK

Allen & Unwin (Publishers) Ltd
Park Lane, Hemel Hempstead, Herts HP2 4TE, UK

Allen & Unwin Australia Pty Ltd
8 Napier Street, North Sydney, NSW 2060, Australia

Allen & Unwin with the
Port Nicholson Press
PO Box 11-838 Wellington, New Zealand

ISBN 0 04 940089 4

Designed by Behram Kapadia
Assisted by Andrew Wilkinson

Editing and captions by Ann Wilson

Picture research by Charlotte Ward-Perkins
assisted by Robert Hersh and Jorge Cachinero,
Centro Ortega y Gasset, Madrid
Picture consultant: Annabel Davies

Printed in Spain by Imago Publishing

CONTENTS

Map of Spain 6

Introduction *by Raymond Carr* 7

1 · The Build-Up 24
1930 to June 1936

2 · Revolt and Revolution 38
July 1936

3 · The Early Months 58
August to September 1936

4 · Assault on Madrid and Internationalism 80
October to November 1936

5 · War of Attrition 102
December 1936 to March 1937

6 · The Basque Country and May Events in Barcelona 114
April to June 1937

7 · Steady Nationalist Advance 130
July to November 1937

8 · Republican Defeats 146
December 1937 to June 1938

9 · The Ebro Offensive 160
July to November 1938

10 · Death of the Republic 174
December 1938 to March 1939

Reading List 191

Picture Acknowledgments 192

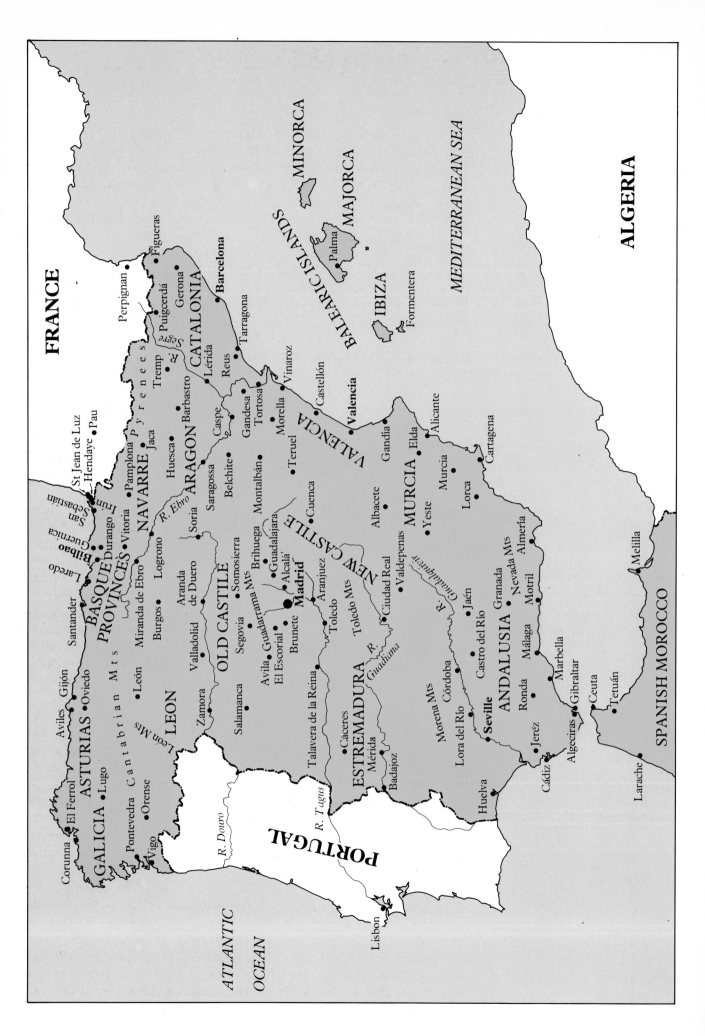

FRANCE

ALGERIA

MINORCA

MAJORCA

MEDITERRANEAN SEA

BALEARIC ISLANDS

IBIZA

Palma

Formentera

Perpignan

Figueras
Gerona
Puigcerdá
CATALONIA
Barcelona
R. Segre
Tremp
Lérida
Tarragona
Reus
Barbastro
ARAGON
Vinaroz
Caspe
Castellón
Jaca
Huesca
Gandesa
Morella
Tortosa
Pamplona
NAVARRE
Saragossa
Belchite
Teruel
VALENCIA
Valencia
St Jean de Luz
Pau
Hendaye
Irún
San Sebastián
Vitoria
Guernica
Durango
BASQUE
PROVINCES
Bilbao
Laredo
R. Ebro
Soria
Montalbán
Gandía
Alicante
Pyrenees
Logrono
Miranda de Ebro
Brihuega
Guadalajara
Cuenca
Albacete
Elda
MURCIA
Cartagena
Santander
Gijón
Aviles
El Ferrol
Corunna
ASTURIAS
Oviedo
Lugo
GALICIA
Pontevedra
Orense
Vigo
Cantabrian Mts
Leon Mts
León
LEON
Zamora
Salamanca
Burgos
Aranda
de Duero
Valladolid
OLD CASTILE
Segovia
Somosierra
Guadarrama Mts
Avila
El Escorial
Brunete
Alcalá
Madrid
Aranjuez
NEW CASTILE
Toledo
Toledo Mts
Ciudad Real
Valdepenas
Murcia
Yeste
Lorca
Almería
Motril
Nevada Mts
Granada
ANDALUSIA
Jaén
Castro del Rio
Córdoba
R. Guadalquivir
Morena Mts
Lora del Rio
Seville
Ronda
Málaga
Marbella
Gibraltar
Algeciras
Ceuta
Tetuán
Jeréz
Cádiz
Huelva
ESTREMADURA
Cáceres
Mérida
Badajoz
R. Guadiana
Talavera de la Reina
R. Tagus
R. Douro
PORTUGAL
Lisbon
ATLANTIC
OCEAN
Melilla
Larache
SPANISH MOROCCO

6

It is not surprising that, fifty years after its outbreak, the Civil War is remembered in Spain not merely for the horrors of the war itself but because it inflicted a deep and long-lasting wound on Spanish society. For it was on his victory in the Civil War that General Franco based his claim to govern Spain: in his view victory in 1939 legitimized a rule that lasted till his death in November 1975, a rule which long denied the defeated in the war any right to participate in public life. It is more surprising, perhaps, that the controversies aroused by the war — the failure of the Western democracies to come to the aid of a sister democracy, the possibility of a popular revolutionary war, the role of the Communist Party — are still alive not only in Europe and the USA but in countries as disparate as Japan and Mexico.

The social cleavages in Spanish society that by July 1936 were to divide the country into two irreconcilable camps, and create repercussions far beyond its frontiers, had become apparent in the early 1930s. The collapse of General Primo de Rivera's dictatorship in 1930 spelt also the collapse of the monarchy. On 12 April 1931 monarchist candidates were soundly beaten in the municipal elections in the cities of Spain. Two days later, King Alfonso left Spain for exile in Rome and the Provisional Government of a Republic was installed to enthusiastic crowd welcome in the streets of Madrid. The new Republic seemed to offer to all but a handful of conservative defenders of the *ancien régime* the prospect of creating a modern democratic society.

However, when the Republican governments set about the task of modernizing Spain, the conflicts in Spanish society came to the fore. To give land to the landless labourers on the great estates of Andalusia, whom Gerald Brenan called the most wretched working class in Europe, was regarded by conservatives as an attack on property. To improve the working conditions of the industrial proletariat in the Catalan factories and in the Basque shipyards and mines was seen by employers as threatening ruin. To give autonomy to Catalonia, for conservative Spanish nationalists was to 'tear Spain to tatters'. To remove the privileges of the Church, above all its control of secondary education, was to Catholics the first step towards the dechristianization of Spain. To reduce the overblown officer corps to reasonable limits was to create military malcontents.

These cleavages became evident in the elections of November 1933. With its slogan 'Religion, Fatherland, Family, Order, Work and Property', the CEDA, a confederation of right-wing Catholic parties led by a compelling mass orator Gil Robles, rallied conservative votes. The Socialists and the Left Republicans had co-operated in Manuel Azaña's government to carry out the modest programme of social reform that seemed to the right 'creeping socialism'. But to the Socialists, bourgeois reformism crept too slowly. They decided to desert the 'Azaña coalition' and Left Republicans and Socialists fought the election as separate parties. Both went down to defeat.

This ushered in the 'Two Black Years', when the CEDA and the conservative Radical Republican party of Alejandro Lerroux, once an anti-clerical firebrand and now a 'tamed lion', attempted to reverse the progressive legislation of the Azaña government. The Socialist party, whose dominant figure was Largo Caballero, a self-educated plasterer and leader of the Socialist union the UGT, regarded the CEDA as Fascists, just as the CEDA regarded the Socialists as Marxist revolutionaries. When the CEDA entered the government in October 1934, the Socialists and the Communists staged an ill-planned rebellion in the mining province of Asturias while the Catalan nationalists, alarmed at the centralism of the conservative government in Madrid, staged a futile rebellion in Barcelona. The Asturias rising was savagely repressed in a military operation directed by the most competent general available: General Franco. Spaniards were already killing each other.

On the emotional surge of an amnesty campaign for the prisoners of the October Revolution, the left gathered strength. The Socialists re-formed their alliance with the Left Republicans of Azaña in the Popular Front, which won the elections of February 1936 — though nearly half of Spain voted for conservative parties. Largo Caballero had, however, supported the Popular Front with reluctance and he refused to join the government formed after the elections, leaving it in the hands of the Left Republicans with their programme of modest social reform. The sober trade union bureaucrat who had spent his life in wage negotiations had been converted to Marxism and the class struggle. He was disabused with bourgeois republicanism, which was unable to effect a socialist transformation of a society still sharply polarized between rich and poor and where agrarian reforms had done little to relieve the lot of the landless labourers. He now wanted a workers' government to replace the bourgeois government of Left Republicans.

This 'bolshevization' of the party was rejected by Indalecio Prieto, a newspaper man and friend of the Left Republicans; it was revolutionary infantilism that could only lead to a Fascist counter-revolution. As for the CNT, the great anarcho-syndicalist union which was a power in Catalonia, Aragon and the Levante, it rejected bourgeois democratic politics *in toto*. The ballot box was a device to deceive the working class; capitalism had feet of clay and it would be smashed by the proletarian revolution.

With Largo Caballero pressing for a workers' government and with the bourgeois Republican government increasingly harassed by strikes and the invasions of estates by landless peasants, the right turned to counter-revolution as the only way to restore 'order'. Gil Robles' 'tactic' — the legal conquest of power to set the Republic on a conservative course — had failed in the February elections. He was not willing to restrain his followers, who saw no alternative to violence and who were joining parties advocating a counter-revolution: Calvo Sotelo's upper-class conservative Nationalists; José Antonio Primo de Rivera's Falange with its mishmash of imported Fascism and Spanish nationalism that would win over the working classes, end the class struggle and establish an anti-capitalist, anti-Marxist, authoritarian corporate state; the Carlists, fervent Catholics in the classic anti-liberal tradition.

Carlists and Falangists, like the proletarian parties, had their uniformed militias. It was the youth of these parties who were absorbing a mystique of violence, and the heady rhetoric now included a voice from the past — an appeal to the army to restore the conservative order in Spain. There was no prospect that the Carlist *requetés*, training in the mountains of Navarre, or the recently outlawed Falangists hiding pistols in their university text books and roughing up their Socialist and Communist counterparts in the streets, could stage a successful counter-revolution. As Calvo Sotelo made clear, this could only triumph if supported by the army.

The army had long developed its own political theory to justify the overthrow of the legal government, putting it into action by the barracks revolt of the *pronunciamiento*. When, in the view of senior officers, corrupt politicians in government had put party before *patria*, when they ceased to represent the general will, when they failed to maintain public order and

Manuel Azaña, Prime Minister and President of the Republic.

left government 'in the gutter', then it was the duty of the army to put the salvation of the *patria* before the 'discipline of lackeys' — that is, obedience to the civil government. Soon after the February 1936 elections, junior officers and a group of generals believed that the time for action had come. General Mola, stationed in Pamplona, sent his agents to the provincial garrisons and the generals in the plot — including General Franco — met in Madrid.

In the years after the Civil War, I asked many of Franco's generals 'Why did you rise on 18 July?' Few believed the Nationalist propaganda line that there was danger of a planned Communist revolution, but they did believe that society was on the verge of some catastrophic disintegration. They had already made plans for a rising when on 13 July the Nationalist leader Calvo Sotelo was murdered by government security agents. This seemed the final proof that violence was uncontainable by a government at the mercy of Largo Caballero, the protagonist of a proletarian take-over bid. Yet Largo Caballero and the CNT were only the rhetoricians of the coming revolution; they had no plans for the translation of rhetoric into action. It was the military revolt, the counter-revolution from above, that was to unleash the revolution from below.

The army rebellion began with the garrisons in Spanish Morocco on 17 July and spread in the next week to the mainland garrisons. It was usually the young officers who took the initiative when their seniors hesitated; those that resisted 'the patriotic and noble national enterprise' of 'our glorious army' were shot. In the south, in Seville, General Queipo de Llano, who was to become famous for his bloodthirsty radio broadcasts, took over the centre of the city with a handful of troops and then wiped out resistance in the working-class quarters. In Galicia, in the extreme north-west, the main cities and the naval base of El Ferrol were captured, and the Civil Guards easily overcame resistance in the countryside: about a thousand people were executed by military courts or shot by Falangist 'Brigades of Repression' at the roadside. Old Castile was the fief of the serious, bespectacled General Mola, the organizer of the military conspiracy; in Asturias General Aranda duped the workers' militia, who were sent off to León, and took the capital, Oviedo. General Cabanellas, a bearded Freemason, deceived the workers for a vital day and consequently Saragossa, the second stronghold of the anarchists and capital of Aragon, went over to the Nationalists — as the rebels came to be called in the press.

The rebellion was not, however, joined by the officer corps *in toto*. A majority of the senior officers remained loyal to the Republic, although their loyalty was suspect to the proletarian parties. Moreover, in general, when the Republican Assault Guard opposed the rebellion, it failed. Though the iconography of the early days — photographs of barricades manned by workers in dungarees pointing rifles at imaginary enemies — gave the impression that it was a workers' rising which defeated the military rising, this was not always the case. Saragossa and Vigo, for example, had strong workers' organizations but they could do nothing against armed security forces and the military. Even in Barcelona, it was a combination of improvised popular resistance and action by the loyal security forces that won the day. As General Goded's troops marched to the centre of Barcelona from the barracks in the suburbs, they were held up by CNT militants behind improvised barricades, and on reaching the city centre they were defeated by the Civil Guards — whose commander became the hero of André Malraux's novel *L'Espoir*. In Madrid there was confusion and hesitation: the rebels gathered in the Montaña barracks, which were taken in one of the set-pieces of popular resistance, flashed across the European press.

Improvised 'uniform' for one of the militiamen on a barricade in Madrid.

In the north, the industrial zone of the Basque Provinces remained loyal, not because the Basque Catholic nationalists shared the ideology of the Popular Front, but because the government had promised the Basques a statute of autonomy, similar to that already granted to Catalonia in 1932. In Navarre, however, the Carlist levies arrived in lorries in Pamplona with their red berets and their flags; they provided the only popular mass support for the Nationalist rising.

If the rebels had planned a national take-over bid, a military *pronunciamiento* in the old style, they had failed. The result was civil war. Spain was divided into a 'red' and a 'white' zone by a long, thinly held front; gradually Spaniards realized that they were cut off from each other as telephones, railway trains, letters and road traffic stopped at the frontiers of the zones. As Prieto declared in a broadcast — the radio was for the first time an instrument of war — the balance sheet of resources favoured the Republic. The rebels soon controlled much of conservative, agrarian Spain, but the Republic controlled the industrial heartlands and the gold reserves of the Bank of Spain. The Nationalists had failed to take over the fleet; most of the ships were either in Republican ports or had put to sea and been taken over by the crews.

The rebels, however, had the advantage of the trained African Army which was under the command of General Franco. At the start of the rebellion, he had flown to Morocco from the Canary Islands, in an aeroplane hired in England, in order to take over command there, but initially his troops were locked up in Africa since he dared not risk ferrying them to the mainland in the face of the Republican fleet — inefficient though it was. However, at the end of July, after securing the assistance of Hitler and Mussolini, the troops began to be brought to southern Spain in planes supplied by Germany and Italy. This was the first airlift in modern war and it was to prove decisive. Without the African Foreign Legion and *regulares* (native troops officered by Spaniards), the Nationalists might well have lost the war in the first months. Hitler later remarked that the Nationalists should erect a monument to the Junkers planes.

The first aim of the rebels was to capture Madrid in a pincer movement, with Mola's troops advancing from the north and Franco's army from Andalusia. It was during this advance that the shortcomings for which the Republic was to pay a terrible price became evident. The improvised popular resistance to the rebellion in its early days was much celebrated in Republican propaganda and in the world press, but the improvisations needed to be replaced when it became clear that the Republic was committed to a long, difficult war. Instead, they lingered on.

The political response to the rising in the Republican zone had been the 'spontaneous revolution' — the take-over of local government by a bewildering variety of party and workers' committees. They filled a vacuum. 'The whole state apparatus', wrote Dolores Ibarruri, famous as the Communist Party's most compelling mass orator, 'was destroyed and state power lay in the streets.' When the government authorities' resistance to the rebellion appeared feeble, when mayors and civil governors refused to arm the workers' organizations, those organizations took over effective local power. It was to save Spain from just such a revolution that the generals had justified their action but as the anarchist leader Federica Montseny remarked, 'The generals' rising gave us the revolution we all wanted but had not expected to take place.'

Central government control had already been lost to the committees and organizations of the proletarian parties when the Popular Front government of Professor Giral, made up of left-wing bourgeois Republicans, came to power on the night of 19 July after the stop-gap

José Antonio Aguirre, elected President of the Basque state created in October 1936.

Enlistment poster for the Aragon militia, presented as a peasant army but in fact mostly composed of townspeople.

Warning against careless talk, published by the UGT and CNT as part of the campaign against fifth columnists.

EL RUMOR
¡GUERRA A MUERTE AL RUMOR! QUE INTENTA DESTROZAR NUESTRA MORAL Y NUESTRA UNIÓN

government of Martínez Barrio had failed to negotiate a truce with General Mola. Giral allowed arms to be given to the workers' organizations, which gave them effective power in the streets. Madrid was in the control of the UGT; in Barcelona the Anti-Fascist Militia Committee dominated by the CNT displaced the legal government of the Generalidad under President Companys.

The military response had been the militia system: hastily formed columns of volunteer soldiers dependent on the unions and parties which recruited them and which gave them their often bizarre names. They were increasingly the despair of the loyal regular officers in their attempts to organize resistance. Franco's army on the march to Madrid in the late summer of 1936 cut through the militia units 'like a knife through butter'. At Talavera, the last town on the road to Madrid, the journalist Franz Borkenau found 'not the slightest trace of a unified command in this motley crowd'.

The committees and their corresponding militia commandeered cars, set up 'popular restaurants', organized their own police patrols. It was improvised police 'controls' in the Republican rearguard which were responsible for the notorious *paseos* (taking for a ride): the indiscriminate killings of suspected Fascists and Fifth Columnists — the word was coined by General Mola himself boasting of his Fifth Column of supporters ready to rise in Madrid. Spy mania equally infected the Nationalist rearguard, and reports of executions and atrocities in each zone set off mutual revenge killings, the pornography of civil war.

The 'spontaneous revolution' had further aspects. What might be called its economic and social aims were embodied in the slogan 'collectivization': the take-over of factories and farms by an assortment of workers' committees. Collectivization was most complete in Catalonia where the CNT was strong; even the theatres and music halls of Barcelona were collectivized, with standard wages for all — to the fury of the star actresses. In rural Aragon, the showplace of agrarian collectivization, the great estates and the small peasants were collectivized in what were large agri-businesses, controlled by the CNT Catalan militia.

The merits of the collectives are still a source of bitter controversy. To their defenders on the radical left, they were the great achievement of proletarian voluntarism. To their opponents, they were inefficient; 'collective egoism' split the economy into fragments which made the rational planning of resources impossible and alienated peasant proprietors and the middle classes whose support the Republican cause needed.

Until the autumn of 1936, it was middle-class Republicans who continued to constitute the Popular Front government but on Giral's resignation in early September the UGT leader Largo Caballero became Prime Minister and on 4 November the CNT agreed to join the Cabinet. Representatives of the spontaneous revolution were now in the Popular Front government's ministry and they confronted what Largo Caballero's secretary called the 'supreme task' of re-creating a state machine: ending revolutionary improvisation by establishing the powers of the central government; order in the rearguard; transforming the militia into a regular, disciplined army. This programme was summarized in the slogan 'a single command' — the *mando unico*.

Gustav Regler, a German Communist who fought in Spain, found the atmosphere of revolutionary improvisation in the early days intoxicating but, he concluded, 'hot-blooded unreason . . . could never lead to the construction of an orderly state on any earlier pattern'. Regler was justifying the party line, for the main propagandist of the *mando unico* was the rapidly growing Communist Party. Once the advocates of a Soviet Republic of Workers and Peasants, they now followed the party line set out in the Comintern Congress of 1935: Popular Fronts, including all democrats, against Fascism. The bourgeois alliance implied the postponement of the revolution until the war was won. The party theorists got to work revising Lenin's thesis on the necessity of replacing bourgeois governments by a workers' government: 'Objective historical conditions do not permit a proletarian revolution.' The revolution that is taking place', repeated Dolores Ibarruri, 'is a bourgeois democratic revolution.'

This revised thesis was unacceptable to those anarchists who rejected 'collaborationism' — of which their leadership, by joining a bourgeois government, gave evidence of guilt — and to the Marxist revolutionaries of the POUM, former followers of Trotsky whose strength lay in Catalonia. To them, the war and the revolution were inseparable and their combination the recipe for victory — a position still defended by the new Left and Trotskyites. 'The only dilemma', as the Italian anarchist Camilo Berneri put it, 'is either victory through revolutionary war or defeat.'

While the CNT was divided between revolutionaries and collaborationists, and while Indalecio Prieto and Largo Caballero struggled for control of the Socialist movement, the Communists were disciplined and single-minded. They were a party capable, as Jesús Hernández, a member of the Spanish Politburo, put it, of 'deriving the utmost benefit from their [the Socialists'] suicidal antagonisms'. With political leverage given them as allies of the Soviet Union, the main supplier of arms to the Republic at war, they were a formidable force. They could preach moderation as experienced revolutionaries with the prestige, still undimmed, of a party that had made the only proletarian revolution of the West.

Since Largo Caballero, in spite of his effort to establish the powers of the legitimate government of the Popular Front, did not toe the Communist line as Minister of War, they determined to destroy him. In this they could count on the help of Largo's old enemies, Prieto and President Azaña, who both believed Largo to be a disaster, incapable of dismantling the 'spontaneous revolution' and restoring ordered government by an effective *mando unico*. Republicans, Prieto Socialists and the Communist Party united to destroy him. He had become morose, secretive, a cantankerous schoolmaster rather than the 'Spanish Lenin'.

The pretext for the destruction of Largo Caballero came with the May events of 1937 in Barcelona. Tensions had mounted in the spring as the revolutionaries of the POUM and the anarchist militants had seen 'their' revolution under attack by the Communists and their militia dissolved without protest from the 'collaborationist' leadership. 'Everyone', wrote T.C. Worsley, a naive English observer, 'seemed to be ready at the slightest provocation to start a malicious ugly little row.' When in May the police moved against the Telephone building, occupied by the CNT, sectarian bitterness erupted into violence: what George Orwell, a volunteer with the POUM whose book *Homage to Catalonia* describes those events, called a 'dust up'. Desultory street fighting lasted four days and ended with an uneasy truce by the CNT leaders themselves.

To the Communists, the POUM — hated because of its Trotskyite line and its criticism of the Soviet purge in its paper *La Batalla* — were Fascist collaborators, a *canaille* that must be destroyed. When Largo Caballero refused to believe these slanders and destroy the POUM, they moved against him. On 16 May he was forced to resign and was replaced by Dr Negrín, a physiologist, a man of enormous appetite and bursts of tremendous energy. Negrín was to remain premier to the end of the war; he was not a fellow

Parade of the newly formed Popular Army passing the headquarters of the POUM Youth in Barcelona, February 1937; the placards show (left to right) Colonel Macía, revered leader of the Catalan left who had died in 1933, Prime Minister Largo Caballero, Catalan President Luis Companys and the Republic's President Manuel Azaña.

Ramón Serrano Suñer, Franco's
brother-in-law, appointed his
Minister of the Interior in 1938.

traveller or Communist tool but like the Communists he believed that there
must be a *mando unico* — a concentration of political and military power —
and an end to the collectivists' experiments. By seeking to set government
on the moderate and ordered course elaborated in his Thirteen Points (May
1938), Negrín hoped, in vain as it turned out, that the Western democracies
might come to the aid of a Republican that respected private property.

This distortion of the revolution meant a loss of the impetus of popular
voluntarism, already severely tested by the hardships and shortages of war,
but it did not mean the end of the faction fights. Largo Caballero retired to
his tent but his supporters in the Socialist Youth and in the UGT gave Negrín
a great deal of trouble, and the ruthless campaign of the Communist secret
police against their enemies, which culminated in the assassination in June
1937 of Andrés Nin, leader and theoretician of the POUM, discredited
Negrín at the time and since. Nevertheless, for almost two years he kept the
Popular Front in being, at times worn out by fighting what he called the
despicable plots of his enemies.

All these faction fights became public property. They were reported in
the party newspapers, sometimes in coded language. They were revealed in
provocative posters. Mutual denunciations were often the stuff of orators at
mass meetings. It was contemplating the military effects of this political
fragmentation that General Rojo, the strategic brain of the Republican
Popular Army, concluded that 'Franco won the political war'. Just at the
time when the politicians of the Republic were squabbling, General Franco
was establishing monolithic control over Nationalist Spain.

In the Republic there was never a truly unified command, whereas
Franco had been chosen by his fellow generals in September 1936 to be sole
supreme Commander. His appointment is not surprising. A carefully
orchestrated propaganda campaign had trumpeted his claim to leadership
of the Nationalists. He was a brave and competent officer who had made his
reputation in the Moroccan Wars, and he commanded the African Army,
the finest fighting force on the Nationalist side; although a cautious
participant in Mola's conspiratorial plans — his 'prudence' was turned into
a virtue by Francoist propaganda — he was one of the few generals who had
studied the Communist Party and who believed in the dangers of a
Communist take-over. From a middle-class family, he had married an
upper-class woman and shared the prejudices of that class, particularly its
identification of Catholicism with the essence of Spanish national unity, a
unity now threatened by separatists in Catalonia and the Basque Provinces
and by Jews, free-thinking Masons, 'Reds' and liberals — all fighting for the
Republic. Franco demanded, and was given, more than military command
to combat this threat: he received 'all the powers of the new state'.

But what was the new state of the Nationalists? Franco's brother-in-law,
Serrano Suñer, who had escaped from Madrid, saw that it must be
something more than the rule of the Junta of generals set up in Burgos. It
must have a political structure, and the diverse forces that backed the
Nationalists must be brought into a single party. These forces included the
traditionalist ultra-Catholic Carlists, a variety of conservative politicians
and the Falange.

The Falange was in disarray, overwhelmed by the massive influx of 'new
shirts' and weakened by the rivalries of its local clans. Its founder, José
Antonio Primo de Rivera, was executed on 20 November 1936, to become
the proto-martyr, the 'absent one' of Nationalist Spain, his name and the
Falangist insignia painted on the walls of cathedrals and churches. Apart
from Carlism — a relic of the past — the Falange provided the only
ideological coverage available to the generals, though conservatives like
Franco himself had no liking for its rhetorical social radicalism. In turn, the

Falange's provisional leader, Manuel Hedilla, did not want to see the idealism of the movement swallowed up by military conservatives. Nor were Carlists, who planned to restore a traditionalist monarchy, much more acceptable to Franco, or he to them.

Franco, built up by Nationalist propaganda as the indisputable caudillo, the liberator of Toledo, used a gun-fight between the Falangist clans and the intrigues of the Carlist leader, Fal Conde, to force unity on both groups 'from above'. The Decree of Unification of 19 April 1937 created what was to be called the Movement, which attempted to bridge the gap between the historic Carlist conservatives and the Falange with its radical programme. In effect what was created by the Decree was Francoism, the personal rule of the caudillo. The Carlists, as Fal Conde put it, 'lost the lot'. The Falangists were rewarded by control of the Nationalist Syndicates — the labour organizations intended to create a corporate state in which workers and employers should be integrated in 'vertical' unions, thus ending the class struggle. The radicalism of the Falange vanished when time-servers replaced idealists; the Syndicates became the tame accomplices of the Francoist state. By May 1937 Franco thus possessed, as a French general observed, a 'concentration of power in time of war such as had been realized nowhere since Napoleon'. Franco was to keep these powers long after the war had ended, and the Movement was to remain the sole political organization of Spain until 1976.

Unlike the Popular Front, which lacked a simple unifying ideology apart from resistance to Fascism, the Nationalists found an ideological anchor in the defence of Catholicism, which was seen as consubstantial with Spain itself. The Catholic Church was inevitably a bitter foe of the Republic given the attack on its position by Republican governments and the horrific massacre of priests and nuns, and church burnings in the early days of the war — an explosion of popular anti-clericalism set off by resentment of the Church, which was perceived as the defender of the oppressors of the working class. For the Nationalists, the Civil War became a crusade against the enemies of God: Masons, Jews and Marxists.

From Navarre, the focal point of mass religious commitment, there radiated the brand of fierce orthodoxy and Catholic puritanism that was to mark, for many years to come, the tone of life in Nationalist Spain. It was Navarre that first legislated against shirt-sleeves in cafés and 'immodest' dress in women, campaigned against make-up and instituted (unsuccessfully) 'smokeless days'. It was in Navarre that the orthodoxy of Tridentine Catholicism, fierce in its resistance to all modernizing trends in the Church, first extended its grip over intellectual and social life in an attempt to wipe out the ravages of nineteenth-century liberalism from Spanish life.

In spite of residual traces of Falangism, Franco's new state seemed a re-creation of the Spain of Ferdinand and Isabella with Fascist trimmings. The Generalissimo's war-time headquarters were a reflection of the court of the monarchy. He received the Italian ambassador in the splendid palace of the Salamanca municipality, 'surrounded by a large number of officials and officers, all in uniform — in a room decorated with superb sixteenth-century tapestries and eighteenth-century porcelain brought specially for the occasion from Vitoria'. But behind this facade Nationalist Spain had its own brand of terror used systematically to break resistance in 'liberated' territory; European opinion had first learnt of this as early as August 1936 when Badajoz was captured and savage killings followed. In Nationalist-controlled Galicia, the leader of the Galician nationalists was among those shot after trial in a military court in which he had defended the Galician language. 'Separatists', it was argued, were destroying the unity of Spain

Carlist *requetés*, painted by the Nationalist artist Sáenz de Tejada.

The internationally acclaimed Spanish poet and dramatist Federico García Lorca, killed by Falangists in August 1936.

Homage to Lorca paid at an International Writers' Congress held in July 1937.

that it was the aim of the Nationalist crusade to impose from above.

All this was in sharp contrast to the proletarian flavour of the Republican zone which so moved the European left. George Orwell came to Barcelona in the early days of the war, before the revolution had gone stale and the Communist secret police like some 'huge evil intelligence' had created a 'horrible atmosphere of suspicion and hatred'. He found in the summer of 1936 a city that seemed to have emerged into an era of equality and freedom. 'It was the first time I had ever been in a town where the working class was in the saddle. Practically every building of any size had been seized by the workers and draped with red flags or the red and black flag of the anarchists . . . almost every church had been gutted and its images burnt. Waiters and shop workers looked you in the face and treated you as an equal . . . There were no private motor-cars . . . The revolutionary posters were everywhere . . . Down the Ramblas, the wide central artery of the town where crowds of people streamed constantly to and fro, the loudspeakers were bellowing revolutionary songs all day and far into the night . . . In outward appearance it was a town in which the wealthy class had practically ceased to exist.'

The Republic honoured intellectuals, in contrast to the Nationalists' distrust of them, and paid great attention to education of children. The commissars attached to army units distributed newsletters and conducted a campaign against illiteracy. There were also literacy campaigns in the countryside, and promotion of liberated roles for women. Strange enthusiasms flourished: naturism, a craze for Esperanto. Along with church burnings and anti-clericalism went the anarchists' own brand of puritanism: there was an attempt, unsuccessful, to turn the sleazy music halls of Barcelona to educational purposes and to close down brothels. One result of the Republic's concern for culture was the importance given to posters as a means of sustaining the war effort. Most artists worked in Barcelona and Madrid and they were organized in Barcelona in a Professional Artists' Syndicate; its workshop became a poster factory. Compared with the Republic's posters, those of the Nationalists were mostly poor and conventional.

Again in contrast to the Nationalists and their execution of separatists, the Republic remained a supporter of autonomy for the historic nationalities, the Basques and the Catalans. This, however, increased the difficulties of creating a *mando unico*. Catalan nationalists resented the interference of central government, which did not succeed in establishing its control over the essential war industries of Catalonia until late in the war. Deprived of his power, President Companys retired to the study of Catalan poetry. The Basque nationalists, very dissimilar to the Catalans but equally resentful of central government authority, saw their army as an independent force, and once their homeland, Euzkadi, had been conquered, the war lost its purpose for them. Azaña complained bitterly of the effects of what he called 'cantonalism', the division of the Republican zone into a maze of competing authorities whose independence was reflected in the issue of bank notes to replace the coins that had gone out of circulation.

At the time and since, supporters of the Republic blamed the defeat of democracy in Spain less on political infighting and provincial 'cantonalism' than on the failure of fellow democracies, in particular France and Britain, to send arms to Spain. While Germany and Italy went on providing supplies to the Nationalists, only the Soviet Union gave arms to the Republic, thereby strengthening the grip of the Communists on political life.

France and Britain avoided fulfilling their democratic obligations by adopting the policy of non-intervention — the pledge by the European nations to refuse to supply arms to either side. When the war broke out, Léon Blum and the Popular Front were in power in France, and although Blum wanted to help the Republic with arms supplies, he was faced by the violent reaction of the right, including his Foreign Minister, which would have destroyed the Popular Front government. He therefore accepted the policy of non-intervention as the only available way to help the Republic. In Britain the Conservative government of Stanley Baldwin had no sympathy with what it regarded as a 'red' government in Spain. It was haunted by the fear that intervention would bring a general war and its increasing concern was to patch up relations with Mussolini.

The French and British set up the Non-Intervention Committee, which sat in London from September 1936 and whose members included representatives of the European powers. If the policy had worked, it might have provided, in British Foreign Secretary Anthony Eden's later words, a 'leaky dam', but it did not provide even that. The endless verbal battles — what the Soviet representative on the Committee called 'spaghetti' — did not prevent the Germans and Italians pouring arms into Spain, while paying lip-service to non-intervention.

Both Mussolini and Hitler saw that a Nationalist Spain would be a useful Mediterranean ally against France, and this strategical consideration, rather than any ideological sympathy or pre-existing involvement in the generals' rising, led Hitler to send the Junkers 52s that brought Franco's African Army to Spain. Later, in November 1936, came the Condor Legion, kept at a strength of 100 planes, which gave the Nationalists command of the air in a war where aerial bombardment of ground troops became decisive in battle for the first time. Mussolini's contribution was mainly in aeroplanes, light tanks and lorries, and ground troops, which at their maximum perhaps totalled some 47,000.

With no such generous allies in the West supplying arms on credit — in the German case payment involved handing over the considerable mineral resources of Spain — the Republicans were dependent on Soviet arms supplies, paid for by the gold of the Bank of Spain. Russian heavy tanks arrived in late October 1936, as did Russian fighter planes, which gave the Republic a temporary superiority in equipment. With the arms came Russian military advisers whose interference was often resented by anti-Communist Spanish officers and by Largo Caballero himself, who turned the Soviet Ambassador out of his office. The Soviet supplies had either to come through France or, when the French frontier was closed, face the attacks of Italian submarines. Without them, the Republic would have gone under by early 1937, but they staved off defeat rather than underwrote victory.

Outside the Soviet Union only Mexico gave its support: Spanish intellectuals were given refuge and founded what was to become a most prestigious research institution, the Colegio de Mexico. Democratic America, true to its isolationist traditions, approved of the British support of non-intervention. President Roosevelt introduced legislation to stop the private supply of arms, which was overwhelmingly supported in Congress where only one representative pleaded for the 'legitimate rights of democratic Spain . . . assaulted by the Fascist hordes'. A later attempt by Roosevelt to raise the embargo was shelved through Catholic opposition. Since, however, the Neutrality Act of 1935 did not recognize oil as a vital commodity, Franco was supplied with three million tons on credit from US companies, chiefly Texaco whose president admired Franco; without these supplies it is hard to see how Franco could have kept the war going. British capitalists in turn did their best to weaken the Republic financially, and

Léon Blum, Prime Minister of the Popular Front government in France from June 1936 to June 1937.

Chinese member of the International Brigades in prison in Spain after capture by the Nationalists.

Ernest Hemingway in Spain, January 1938.

business interests based their policies on the desirability of a Franco victory.

Although it could not compare with the pilots and troops supplied by Germany and Italy, the Republic did have a supply of men from abroad: the International Brigades. They were not technically sent by the Soviet Union but were volunteers whose recruitment was organized by the Comintern agencies in Paris. Their hard core was made up of political refugees who had seen Fascists stamp out the left in their own countries: men like the German Communist Gustav Regler and the Italian Liberal Pacciardi; Polish miners working in Belgium; Czech, Hungarian and Yugoslav militants; workers' leaders from all over Europe who had sought refuge in the Soviet Union and now hoped — in vain — for an independent role in Western Europe.

The publicity given to the presence of intellectuals such as Ralph Fox, the Cambridge poet, obscured the fact that most volunteers were ordinary workers, fighting alongside the core of committed Communist militants, hardened in the class struggle. The French contingent was composed largely of factory workers and at some 10,000 members constituted about a quarter of the total Brigade strength. The British contingent was less politically homogeneous, less proletarian; their motives were mixed: idealism, unemployment, and sheer boredom with a depressed and depressing Britain. 'I happened to be in Ostend at the time', wrote one volunteer, 'and was bored to desperation.' Most of them nevertheless felt, however dimly, that they were fighting against Fascism. Jason Gurney, a convivial sculptor and habitué of King's Road pubs, thought that 'by fighting against Fascism in Spain, we would be fighting against it in our own country, and every other'.

Recruitment to the Brigades began in the early autumn of 1936 and was at its height over the following six months. In February 1937 the Lincoln Brigade arrived from America, including in its number the only Japanese national to volunteer; he had left his ship in New York and become a minor figure in Labour politics — the world from which many American Brigaders were recruited.

Once in Spain, idealism underwent a severe test. The Brigades were often controlled by humourless Communists, more inclined to hunt out political dissidents than to provide for the creature comforts of the men. When Jason Gurney's battalion arrived at the front, 'bread was scarce and always stale . . . at no time was any attempt made to consider the welfare of the men. Owing to the absence of washing facilities for either person or clothing, the entire battalion became infested with body lice.'

Like the militia, the Brigades were at first sent into battle after a few days' barrack training, at the base camp at Albacete, sometimes without rifle practice for lack of arms. Not surprisingly some of their early actions were disastrous, with officers wandering about looking for troops and transport. The Lincoln Brigade was flung into the battle of Jarama almost on its arrival in Spain and suffered terrible losses under an incompetent commander. Only fierce discipline turned a polyglot force — it used an invented Franco-Spanish *lingua franca* — into units that could be sent into difficult actions.

The imagination of the left was particularly moved by the International Brigades, which received pep-talks, propaganda and visits from, among others, J.B.S. Haldane, Henri Cartier-Bresson, Ernest Hemingway, Clement Attlee and Errol Flynn — though they could do little to satisfy the standard grouses of soldiers. Nationalist propaganda also made a great deal of the Brigades, but although perhaps 40,000 men served in them, their maximum strength at any one time was probably 20,000 and after December 1936 there were always more Italians and Germans in Spain than International Brigaders. By mid-1937 recruitment had fallen off and it became increasingly difficult to ferry the volunteers to Spain. The gaps in the battalions were filled by Spanish conscripts.

On the Nationalist side there was no Comintern to organize an international volunteer force. The German combatants were not volunteers, nor did they feel committed in the same way as did the best spirits in the International Brigades. Galland, the German air ace, though he shared the common 'anti-bolshevik' feelings of his class, felt not for Spain but for the greatness of the new German air force. Whereas the Internationals were seen off at stations with demonstrations and greeted as heroes in Spain, the German pilots were slipped in secretly and, it was hoped, unobserved.

Volunteers to the Nationalist cause came as individuals, often wandering from Burgos to Salamanca and finding it hard to get attached to a Nationalist unit. The only organized — if that is the word — contingent was General O'Duffy's Irish Brigade. Whatever fighting qualities it may have had were ruined by its commander's political ambitions and his propensity for hard liquor; the Brigade was shipped home having had little opportunity to fight in the Crusade.

Injured men of General O'Duffy's Irish Brigade arriving in Dublin, June 1937.

Foreign arms and foreign 'technicians' notwithstanding, the war remained a pauper's war. Neither side had all the modern weapons it wanted, when it wanted them; both sides were supplied with enough foreign arms to keep the war going. Long stretches of front were held by a few troops with antiquated and worn-out weapons. At the Jarama battle of early 1937, the International Brigades' machine-guns were described by one who used them as 'a job lot of junk'. The Foreign Legion was one of the best-equipped units on the Nationalist side, yet until the Aragon offensive of 1938 it was equipped with old machine-guns whose firing-pins broke time and time again. A new aeroplane from Italy, a warm jersey or good goggles from English friends, a battery of anti-aircraft guns or a cargo of wheat from Russia were the cause of great rejoicing. It was vastly different from the war of 1939. A concentration of 200 tanks was achieved with difficulty for a major battle; the Germans conquered France with 2,500.

British International Brigade post-war commemoration.

Air forces remained modest. No Spanish fighters were equipped with radio, which gave dog-fights a 1914-18 flavour. Heavy aerial bombardment against ground troops produced collapses of morale — the Spanish pilots claim to have invented dive-bombing — but there was little strategic bombing. Both sides bombed civilian populations, the Nationalists more consistently. Madrid was raided after August 1936, Barcelona and the Mediterranean ports in 1938. These were the first air raids since the relatively minor German raids in the 1914-18 war and in Barcelona the raiders met with neither effective anti-aircraft fire nor fighters. The effects of the raids were therefore observed with interest in a Europe where many felt a greater war was coming. When Guernica was destroyed by fire-bombs in April 1937, the *Manchester Guardian* warned that Manchester would be next on the list. The air raids did not, however, result in mass panics, and heavy casualties from high explosives could be avoided by adequate shelters. In Madrid the bombing produced a reaction of resistance, though the heavier bombings of Bilbao and Barcelona weakened further a morale already severely strained by semi-starvation.

It is remarkable that the war dragged on till 1939, given the political feuds in the Republic, which a survivor described as 'the constitutional vice of the left', and the superior arms deliveries to the Nationalists. After the defeat of the early days, Republican resistance stiffened when the militia system was replaced by the Mixed Brigades of the Popular Army. Though some militia units remained in being till the end of the war, the Popular

MADRID 1936

¡NO PASARAN! ¡PASAREMOS!
e kommen nicht durch! Wir kommen durch!

Photomontage by the German
Socialist John Heartfield, using
Madrid's famous 'No pasaran'
slogan.

Army was a regular army with pay, uniforms and an established hierarchy
of command, composed of militia men who volunteered for the new units
and enlisted men. It showed remarkable powers of resistance and could
stage remarkable offensives against weakly held fronts, but stuck after a
successful initial advance. Its weakness was a scarcity of middle-rank
trained officers — and there lay the superiority of Franco's army.

If the Nationalists had succeeded in their first aim to capture Madrid, the
war might have ended in 1937, but when Franco's troops arrived in the
western suburbs of the capital in November 1936, they were met by the
resistance of the newly formed Mixed Brigades of the Popular Army
organized by Colonel Rojo and rushed to the front. General Miaja became
the popular hero of the city's defence. The slogan — 'They shall not pass' —
an imitation of the slogan of Verdun — became a symbol of popular
resistance to Fascism. 'Here in Madrid', the Republican radio repeated, 'is
the universal frontier that separates liberty and slavery. It is here in Madrid
that two incompatible civilizations are struggling.' The government, which
believed that Madrid would fall, fled to Valencia, but the Nationalist
offensive stalled in the fierce fighting in University City where the
International Brigades went into action for the first time.

Abandoning an expensive frontal attack, Franco sought to cut through
the flanks and isolate the city in the first real battles of the war. The
Nationalist offensive was halted in the battle of Jarama, February 1937,
where the International Brigades suffered appalling casualties. In the
following month, an Italian attack was held at the battle of Guadalajara
which, to Hemingway, was one of the 'decisive battles of the world';
captured prisoners were proof to everyone of the extent of Italian
intervention. These defensive battles proved the mettle of the new army; as
the German ambassador noted, a Nationalist victory was a distant prospect
given Franco's 'slowness'.

After the assault on Madrid had failed, Franco transferred the bulk of
his army to the north. Slowly and methodically, the Nationalist troops,
superior in aircraft and artillery, advanced through the difficult terrain.
The destruction of the Basque market town of Guernica on 26 April with
high explosive and incendiary bombs dropped by German planes of the
Condor Legion shocked world opinion, though for years Francoist
propaganda maintained that the town was destroyed by retreating
anarchists. When it was followed in June by the fall of Bilbao, the industrial
capital of Biscay, the Basque nationalists ensured that the industrial
equipment of their *patria* passed intact to the Nationalists. Once their
homeland had fallen, the war lost its point for them. By the end of the year
Franco had 'liberated' Santander and Asturias, which meant the loss to the
Republic of a rich industrial and mining zone. Though not apparent at the
time to the German and Italian ambassadors who feared Franco's
'slowness', it was the tip of the balance. Only huge arms supplies would save
the Republic.

General Rojo, in a vain attempt to divert Franco from his northern
conquest, had mounted the most ambitious offensive of the war at Brunete
in July 1937. Like all his offensives, it was well planned and achieved total
surprise; 80,000 men and 200 tanks broke the front held by 2,400 troops. It
then bogged down, allowing Franco to bring up his reserves. The story was
repeated at Teruel in December 1937, a terrible winter battle; at Brunete
field telephone lines had burnt on the ground from the extreme heat; at
Teruel sentries froze to death.

Rather than turning his armies gathered round Teruel against
Catalonia, the seat of the Republic's remaining war industry, Franco chose

to drive to the sea; by April 1938 he had succeeded in his aim of dividing the Republican zone in two when he reached the Mediterranean at Vinaroz. But he had committed his armies to a difficult campaign in Aragon. To relieve pressure on Valencia, the Republican General Staff mounted the most ambitious operation of the whole war: the crossing of the River Ebro to take the Francoists in the rear. Again after a brilliant start in July, the battle became a slogging match, a war of attrition won by Franco's superiority in planes and guns. In November the exhausted Republican army withdrew across the Ebro.

Victory in Catalonia would be final victory and Rojo tried desperately to patch together an army. It broke. Unlike heroic Madrid, Barcelona did not put up any resistance. The will to fight had gone; the population was by now half-starved and stunned by daylight bombing raids. The defeated troops poured over the Pyrenean passes to France. I have never forgotten their dejected faces behind the barbed wire of the camps to which they were consigned.

Even after these terrible defeats Negrín believed that he must fight on with the Army of the Centre. Some sudden twist in European politics might bring the democracies to their senses and cause them to resist the advances of Fascism in Spain. The Republican propaganda campaign in the last months was no longer for victory but for resistance. In Madrid, citizens listening to the forbidden Francoist radio could trace the Nationalist advances. Without proper heating to combat the winter, hopelessly undernourished — except for those who had friends in the country or contacts with the flourishing black market — their only relief was the cinema. For the soldiers at the front, the war was like all wars: bad food, long journeys in run-down trains; desertions had become a serious problem.

It was a bitter irony of the Civil War that it ended in a civil war within the Republican camp: a *pronunciamiento* by Negrín's political enemies who disliked his reliance on the Communists and regarded his determination to resist as suicidal. Colonel Casado rose to save Spain from Negrín's misgovernment and what he believed to be a Communist take-over bid, just as the Generals had risen on 18 July to save Spain from the government of the gutter and a 'red' Spain. Casado and his allies hoped that Franco would sign an agreement with such fervent anti-Communists that would save loyalists from reprisals, but Casado troops fought the Communist units in Madrid in vain. Franco had no other intention than to exact a heavy punishment for all those who had not supported the Movement. He refused anything but unconditional surrender. The Republican armies disintegrated. At the end of March Francoist troops entered the grey and exhausted city of Madrid in triumph. On 1 April 1939 the caudillo of Spain, which in his own terminology he had liberated, declared that the war was over.

In the end victory had gone to a better disciplined, better equipped army where the 'provisional lieutenants' trained by regular officers and German experts provided the middle leadership that the Republicans so often lacked. The heroism and competence of the best units of the Popular Army could not finally match an army where the *mando unico* was in the hands of a methodical strategist who was also a military dictator.

As the war became, through the politics of non-intervention, part of the power conflicts of Europe, so this involvement gave Spanish issues an international significance, a contest between the ideologies that divided the continent — democracy and fascism. To Hans Beimler, a German Communist killed fighting with the International Brigades on the Madrid front, it seemed that 'the only way we can get back to Germany is through

Indian Congress Party leader Jawaharlal Nehru, accompanied by his daughter, the future Prime Minister Indira Gandhi, on a visit to Spain in 1938 to show support for the Republic. They are escorted by the Catalan President Luis Companys.

The funeral of German Communist Hans Beimler in Barcelona, autumn 1936.

Madrid'. Lloyd George hoped that the resistance of Republican Spain would 'save European democracy' from the designs of its enemies and the cowardice of its friends. In Latin America, the left-wing supporters of President Cardeñas saw the struggle of the Republic against 'old Spain' as part of their own struggle against old Mexico. 'General Cardeñas', ran the posters, 'defeated at Teruel.'

A process of identification with one or other of the two combatants transformed the war into a dividing line in domestic politics and intellectual discourse. Bitter political divisions were created in Britain and France. The British Labour Party attacked the Conservatives for their support of the farce of non-intervention. Yet the Labour Party itself was divided between the left of the Party, which pressed for aid to Spain through a United Front with the Communists, and the right, which included leaders like Ernest Bevin who distrusted the Communists and sensed that the British working class did not want to go to war over Spain. Bevin rammed home the paradox that the left who wanted aid to Spain were at the same time pacifists opposing rearmament. The divisions that the Civil War created in British politics were not healed until the 1939 war superseded them. In France, partly because of the presence of Spanish exiles and their role in the resistance, the wounds did not heal.

Whatever the divisions revealed by the Spanish war, its impact on writers and intellectuals was tremendous. With few exceptions — Catholics such as Evelyn Waugh, the poet Roy Campbell, inhabitants of ivory towers like T.S. Eliot — most writers were broadly liberal. They saw in the support of the Republic at war the 'last cause'. That their commitment was ruthlessly organized and exploited by Communists, or that it was often emotionally and psychologically self-regarding, should not blind us to its genuine nature.

All over the world men responded to this call precisely because they were liberals of one sort or another, shocked at the overthrow of a 'progressive' government. John Kennedy, in spite of family Catholicism, recognized that the Republican government was 'right, morally speaking'; that 'its program was similar to the New Deal'.

To help the Spanish resistance gave a generation of intellectuals in Britain, beaten down by the depression, unemployment and the National Government, the sensation of effective action. A sense of personal liberation can be felt in most of the writing on the Civil War. Before the inexorable end came in sight, intellectuals felt on the side of history for once; they identified with Spaniards 'fighting for freedom'. It is an uncomfortable phenomenon of identification in some ways. Gustav Regler, who joined the International Brigades, observed: 'Only on this occasion have I known that sense of freedom and feeling of unconditional escape, of readiness for absolute change . . . We don't write history now, we make it.' The time when the Republic looked like winning was to Hemingway and his friends, 'the happiest period of our lives'. 'You are all bad, growled Ezra Pound, more concerned about the ravages of usury than the issues at stake in the war, 'Spain is an emotional luxury to a gang of dilettantes.'

The war indeed posed in an acute form the social and political responsibility of the author. Whether the total commitment of writers produced great literature is another matter. To Cecil Day Lewis, the English poet, the war was simply 'a battle between light and darkness'. There was no place for the tender liberal conscience. 'You must say yes or no to Fascism', said Koltsov, the Soviet journalist — which meant accepting his condemnation of left-wing dissidents as Trotskyites.

It was in France that the intellectual and political repercussions of the war were most intensely felt. The Communist Party was powerful and its

connections with French intellectuals much more intimate than in Britain, where the Party was miniscule and its intellectuals suspect. Paris was the centre of Willi Muenzenberg's exertions in organizing front groups and propaganda drives. Hence the French Party's onslaught on non-intervention — the policy of a Socialist, Léon Blum — was bitter. The French Popular Front, weakened, dissolved in recrimination.

Apart from those who gave their lives in the war, such as the English poet Cornford, the fate of those who committed themselves to the Republic was often tragic. In the Soviet Union contact with the West was always dangerous. In the army purge of 1937 only Malinovsky escaped of the military advisers in Spain. To have been in Spain also proved fatal to some Czech Communists after 1951. 'Service in the Brigades' became synonymous with 'Trotskyite activities' or service in the American intelligence network. 'Your whole group is in the bag', his interrogator told the Czech Brigader Arthur London. 'Now we know what veterans from Spain really are.'

The experience of the Lincoln Brigaders and their sympathizers in the United States forms an interesting parallel. During the war, once the Soviet Union had become an ally in the struggle against Fascism, Lincoln Brigaders and Spanish Republican refugees were on the right side. In the McCarthy period they became suspect and were harassed. It is ironical that Lincoln Brigaders who stuck to their ideals and memories fell into the same category as Czech Communist volunteers. 'The only way of proving your loyalty towards the Party', as a Czech interrogator put it in the Slansky trial, 'is to adapt yourself to its present means of judging past events.' But there were Czechs like London and obscure Lincoln Brigaders who could not and would not deny their pasts.

The response of the right did not involve such complexities. Franco found conservative apologists, the most extreme of whom were prepared to call him 'perhaps a saint' and to swallow the 'red plot' as an explanation of the immediate origins of the war. Catholics, with notable exceptions, accepted the vision of the war as a crusade. In the United States, however, a considerable proportion of the American Catholic laity did not follow their bishops — an indication of the strength of the American progressive tradition.

For many in America and Britain, the Spanish problem posed dilemmas that were real enough. How could pacifist Socialists, who were fighting rearmament, advocate a degree of support for the Spanish Republic which might entail a general war? How could Roosevelt, who came to regard his arms ban on Republican Spain as a moral error, attack non-intervention when his whole policy depended on friendship with France and Great Britain, the creators and proponents of non-intervention? How could American Jewish liberals — Goebbels had said that all Jews supported the Republic — and Negroes demand from the administration a stand against Franco when it was the Catholic vote which had helped to bring their standard-bearer, Roosevelt, to the White House? How could liberal Catholics support the conquerors of Ethiopia and those who had brought about the decline and fall of the League of Nations?

Moreover, those in the literary and political establishment were uneasily conscious that their own passionate obsession was not shared by the majority. Bevin sensed the shallowness of the general reaction of the British working class which, as George Orwell was to observe, 'saw their Spanish comrades slowly strangled and never aided them by a single strike'. True, they raised money for Spain; but their contributions 'would not equal five per cent of the turnover of the football pools'.

The consequences of the involvement of intellectuals of the left are

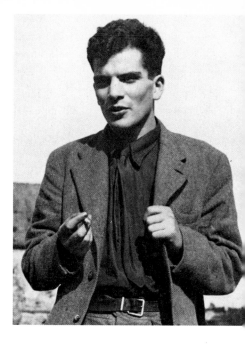

The Cambridge poet John Cornford in Spain.

American relief organization booklet of 1938 appealing for sympathy with the Republic's plight.

The Hungarian-born English writer Arthur Koestler on his arrest in Spain as an alleged Communist spy in 1937.

reflected, in many cases, in the apoliticism and disillusionment of the writers of the forties. Both Orwell and Arthur Koestler were nauseated by 'the screaming lies and hatred', the use of intellectuals — as happens in any war — for propaganda purposes. It was the activists rather than the writers who carried on the revolutionary tradition. They fought in the French Resistance; Tito, who had organized the flow of Yugoslav volunteers to Spain, later used them to staff his National Liberation Army. It was a Spanish veteran who gave Fidel Castro the elements of his military training.

While for the nations of Europe, the issues of the Spanish Civil War which had divided them were pushed into the background by the greater conflicts of the Second World War, for Spain Franco's victory was a tragedy. It meant nearly forty years of authoritarian rule. To the Republicans in exile, still bitterly divided after the war between the Communists and anti-Communists, the victorious democracies of post-war Europe behaved no better than during the Civil War itself. It needed more than an international boycott, imposed to punish Franco for his collaboration with his supporters Hitler and Mussolini in the Second World War, to bring down a fiercely repressive regime. With the onset of the cold war Franco became, in 1953, the respectable ally of the United States which accepted him on his own terms as the 'Sentinel of the West'. After the executions and imprisonments of the 1940s, buttressed by this international respectability and by the prosperity which came in the 1960s as a striking contrast to the 'years of hunger' after the Civil War, the dictatorship could survive until the death of its creator in November 1975.

It was the Franco regime itself that did not allow the memory of the Civil War to fade away and kept alive the divisions it created. With democracy firmly established, it is only in the minds of the nostalgics of the right that the gulf between the conquered and the conquerors of the Civil War persists. It is the political heirs of the conquered who now rule Spain.

'They shall not pass'; woodcut by Hungarian artist Ernö Berda, 1939, symbolizing the Republic's determined resistance.

1 · The Build-Up

1930

January   General Primo de Rivera, dictator since 1923, dismissed.

August   Republicans and Socialists make Pact of San Sebastian to overthrow monarchy.

December   Republican military rising fails.

1931

April 12   Municipal elections result in sound defeat of monarchists in the cities.

April 14   Proclamation of Second Republic. King Alfonso XIII goes into exile. Alcalá Zamora becomes Prime Minister of provisional government.

June 28   Elections to Cortes; left-wing majority returned.

July   Strike by anarcho-syndicalist trades union, CNT, results in clashes with Socialists in Madrid, Seville and centres countrywide.

October   Alcalá Zamora resigns over Article 26 of new constitution attacking church privileges. Manuel Azaña becomes Prime Minister.

November   Gil Robles becomes head of Catholic conservative party, Acción Nacional (later called Acción Popular).

December   Alcalá Zamora elected President of Republic; Azaña becomes Prime Minister of coalition government of Left Republicans and Socialists. First issue of monarchist journal *Acción Español.*

1932

January   Anarchist rising in Llobregat Valley in Catalonia. Jesuit order dissolved; divorce legalized.

August   General Sanjurjo's military rising in Seville fails.

September   Catalonia is granted autonomy, with its own flag, language and government. Agrarian reform bill passed.

1933

January   Revolt in Barcelona of anarcho-syndicalist CNT/FAI. Agrarian disturbances, which continue through year. Massacre of anarchists in Casas Viejas (Cadiz) by civil guards.

March   Confederation of Catholic right-wing parties, CEDA, founded; led by Gil Robles.

May   Religious reform bill passed, envisaging lay education and closure of church schools.

October   Falange, authoritarian right-wing party, founded under leadership of José Antonio Primo de Rivera. Martínez Barrio becomes Prime Minister of caretaker government to preside over coming elections.

November   Socialists and Left Republicans of Azaña coalition part company. General elections result in right-wing victory over a divided left.

December   Anarchist uprisings and general disturbances. Alejandro Lerroux, leader of conservative Radical Republican party, becomes Prime Minister with CEDA support but no CEDA Cabinet members.

(continued on page 32)

The proclamation of the Second Republic on 14 April 1931 was greeted with widespread enthusiasm. Big political campaigns throughout Spain had led up to the municipal elections of 12 April, which resulted in the heavy defeat of monarchist candidates in the cities. In Madrid *(below and opposite)*, Republican canvassing had been particularly strong and the crowds wildly rejoiced victory while King Alfonso and his family left the capital for exile in Rome.

Left: The new Republic portrayed symbolically.

Below left: The English-born Queen Victoria Eugenia leaving Spain for exile on 15 April 1931.

Below right: Prime Minister Manuel Azaña with Catalan military officers in Lerida, September 1932. The army reforms introduced by Azaña, leader of the government of Left Republicans and Socialists from October 1931 to September 1933, created considerable resentment among the over-staffed officer class.

General Sanjurjo's Rising

In August 1932 General Sanjurjo, commander of the Civil
Guard and hero of the Moroccan Wars, led a military rising in
Seville against the Republic on behalf of conservative and
monarchist forces *(above).* It was timed to coincide with a rising
in Madrid, which was very quickly suppressed. Sanjurjo's rising
failed and he was arrested, tried and sentenced to life
imprisonment. After a short period in prison *(right),* he was
reprieved under the amnesty law of 1933, to become a leader of
the 1936 rising.

AGRARIAN UNREST

The agrarian reform bill of September 1932 did little to solve the acute need for land reform. In much of Spain, the soil was poor and farming methods primitive; poverty and illiteracy were rife, particularly in the south, where millions of landless labourers barely scratched a living from seasonal work on the great estates, often owned by absentee landlords. Strikes and disturbances were increasingly common, including outbursts of anti-clericalism, though the peasantry - as the population as a whole - was nominally Catholic.

Below: Peasant woman at work.
Right above: Cardinal Segura, who was thrown out of Spain after his public attacks on the Republic, greeting villagers in Estremadura, one of the poorest parts of the country.
Right below: Civil Guards escorting a prisoner after the anarchist rising of January 1933 in Casas Viejas, in the province of Cadiz. The rising was viciously suppressed by the newly created Assault Guards sent in under Colonel Rojas, and many prisoners were executed in cold blood.

The Falange

The quasi-Fascist Falange movement was founded in October 1933 under the leadership of Andalusian lawyer José Antonio Primo de Rivera, who entered politics to vindicate the memory of his father, General Primo de Rivera, dictator of Spain from 1923 to 1930. The Falange merged in early 1934 with the right-wing JONS, adopting the latter movement's yoke and arrows emblem.

Right: General Primo de Rivera with his sister and children. José Antonio stands *(second from left)* next to his father; Pilar *(seated right)* later became founder and leader of the women's section of the Falange.

Left: Idealistic portrayal of José Antonio Primo de Rivera, wearing the blue shirt of the Falangists and displaying the movement's insignia.

Below: José Antonio reviewing Falangist youths.

Revolution in Asturias

The miners of Asturias rose in a well-organized rebellion in early October 1934. General Franco (*below*, right, with Major Doval) was seconded by the Ministry of War to organize its suppression, which was carried out with marked brutality under Major Doval. Over a thousand rebels were killed and many more were taken prisoner.

(continued from page 25)

1934

January   Left wins Catalan regional elections; right predominates in rest of Spain. Moderate Socialists lose control of the party, which becomes increasingly revolutionary under influence of Largo Caballero.

February   Falange merges with right-wing JONS party.

March   General strike begins in Saragossa, making anarchist leader Buenaventura Durruti a national figure. At a meeting in Rome Mussolini agrees to support monarchist uprising with weapons and money.

April   Sanjurjo and fellow-conspirators given amnesty.

June   Agricultural workers' strike in southern Spain. Street fighting in Madrid. Catalan and Basque protests against central government.

October: Lerroux forms new, right government that includes CEDA members. Miners' revolution in Asturias, brutally crushed with help of Foreign Legion. Catalan nationalist insurrection in Barcelona fails.

1935

May   After continuing government crises, Lerroux re-forms Cabinet with more CEDA members; Gil Robles becomes War Minister. General Franco appointed Chief of Staff.

June   Luis Companys and fellow Catalan ministers sentenced to penal colony for part in October rising.

July   Comintern's 7th Congress in Moscow approves Popular Front tactics, which become policy of Spanish Communist Party.

September   Revolutionary Marxist party, POUM, formed from two Communist groupings of Andrés Nin and Joaquín Maurín.

December   Preparation for general election after constant government problems and scandals involving Radicals.

1936

January   Left Republicans, Socialists and Communists make Popular Front electoral pact on moderate programme of social reform and amnesty for those involved in October rising.

February   General election results in Popular Front victory. Socialists, now divided between moderate Indalecio Prieto and Largo Caballero and his maximalist policies, do not join government of Left Republicans under Prime Minister Azaña. Franco relieved of command and sent to Canary Islands.

March   Falange banned and Primo de Rivera arrested. Church sackings; right-left street fighting. Socialist-led land seizures in Estremadura.

April   Socialist-Communist youth movements merge in JSU. Cortes dismisses President Alcalá Zamora.

May   General strikes and demonstrations in major cities. Prieto warns of danger of military insurrection. Azaña becomes President and Left Republican Casares Quiroga Prime Minister after Prieto's candidature rejected by Largo Caballero.

June   Building strike begins in Madrid. Plans for military rising furthered under General Mola.
Léon Blum heads Popular Front government in France.

Rising in Catalonia

A Catalan nationalist rising against the central government on 6 October 1934 was quickly suppressed after street fighting in Barcelona *(below)*. President Luis Companys *(above*, centre - with pocket handkerchief) was arrested along with his ministers.

Gil Robles and the CEDA

The CEDA, a confederation of right-wing, Catholic parties formed in 1933, was led by Gil Robles *(left, insert)*. He became War Minister in May 1935 in the conservative Radical Republican government of Alejandro Lerroux, which attempted during the 'Two Black Years' of 1933-35 to reverse the progressive legislation of the Azaña government.

Left: Poster announcing a Gil Robles rally in the bull arena of Madrid, November 1935, in the run-up to the February 1936 elections.

February 1936 Elections

Left Republicans, Socialists and Communists formed a Popular Front to fight, and win, the general elections of February 1936, rallying support through a call for amnesty of those imprisoned for their part in the October 1934 risings.

Right: Catalan election poster by Arteche for the left-wing Catalan nationalist party, Esquerra: 'True order does not exist without collective welfare.'

Below: Communist posters published in Madrid *(left)* and Seville *(right)* using the amnesty campaign to urge people to vote for the Popular Front.

Above: Queuing in the fishworkers' district of Barcelona to vote in the February 1936 elections; women had been able to vote for the first time in 1933.
Below: Prisoners of the October 1934 rising leaving jail in Barcelona after the amnesty granted by the new Popular Front government of February 1936.

Right: Street fighting in Madrid, in October 1934 during the nationwide disturbances *(above)*, and on the fifth anniversary of the Second Republic, April 1936 *(below)*, when there was a pitched battle between Falangists and Assault Guards following violent demonstrations by the Falange and the Socialist youth movement. It was part of the escalating violence throughout Spain involving right and left groups, while the government continued in crisis, with Indalecio Prieto prevented from becoming premier by his Marxist rival, Largo Caballero.

Civil guard and workers fighting alongside to put down the generals'
rebellion; painting by Sim, 1936, published by the propaganda offices of
the revolutionary workers' organization CNT/FAI, which took over
effective control of Barcelona in the first days of the rising.

2 · Revolt and Revolution

1936

July 12   Lt José Castillo, officer of Republican Assault Guards, assassinated by Falangists.

July 13   Calvo Sotelo, leader of right-wing monarchists, murdered in revenge.

July 17-20   Risings in Morocco and throughout Spain.

   17-19   *Morocco* Military coup in Melilla (17th). By end 18th, Ceuta, Tetuán and Larache also taken. Franco flies from Tenerife to Tetuán (19th) to take command of Army of Africa.

   18-20   *Seville* General Queipo de Llano wins town for rebels, who also capture Cádiz, Algeciras and Jeréz.

   18-20   *Madrid* Casares Quiroga resigns; President Azaña asks Martínez Barrio to form moderate government to negotiate with rebel leaders. Street demonstrations. Barrio resigns to be replaced by Left Republican José Giral, who authorizes arming of people's militias and appeals to French Republic for arms. Uncoordinated rebellion put down by enthusiastic workers backed by security forces; churches sacked and burnt; Montaña barracks besieged and rebel inmates slaughtered.

   19-20   *Barcelona* Rebellion put down due to initiative of CNT and POUM and loyalty of security forces; churches looted and burned; Atarazanas barracks besieged. General Goded, arriving from Majorca to lead rising, captured. Anti-Fascist militias formed.

   19-20   *Pamplona* General Mola imposes martial law and dispatches rebel troops to Madrid.

   19   General Aranda seizes Oviedo for rebels.

July 20   General Sanjurjo killed in plane crash on way from Lisbon to Burgos to head the Nationalist cause. British Labour Party expresses its backing of the Republic; government under Stanley Baldwin remains uncommitted.

July 21   Beginning of two-month siege of Alcázar in Toledo, where rebels under Colonel Moscardó have taken refuge. Rising at Almería crushed.

July 22   General Mola's forces reach Somosierra Pass in Guadarrama mountains north of Madrid. Most of Galicia held by rebels.

July 23   Governing council for rebel-held territory, Junta de Defensa Nacional, set up at Mola's headquarters in Burgos. Rebellion at Alicante defeated. Catalan Communists and Socialists merge in PSUC.

July 24   Rebels take Granada.

July 25   Rebel columns from Vallodolid and Salamanca capture Alto de Léon pass to north-west of Madrid. Catalan militia columns head for Aragon. First shipment of French planes crosses border.

July 26   Comintern agrees to seek volunteers and funds to help Republic. Hitler agrees to Franco's request for military aid.

July 28   German planes arrive in Morocco to begin airlift of Army of Africa troops into Seville.

July 30   People's militias attack army barracks in Valencia. Italian planes arrive in Morocco.

Front-page headlines of the ABC newspaper on 20 July 1936: 'Long Live Spain' *(above)* in rebel-controlled Seville, where General Queipo de Llano had seized power, and 'Long Live the Republic' *(below)* in Madrid, which remained loyal to the government.

The Generals' Plot

Plans for a military rising against the Republic had been seriously under way since spring 1936, organized by General Mola in Pamplona. General Sanjurjo was to fly into Spain from Portugal, where he had been living since his release from prison. General Franco, stationed by the government in the Canary Islands, was to take command of the Army of Africa in Morocco. The rising was precipitated by the assassination on 12 July of Lt José Castillo of the Assault Guards, followed the next day by the revenge murder of the right-wing monarchist leader, Calvo Sotelo.

Left: Franco with a Moorish chieftain during the Moroccan campaigns of the 1920s when he made his reputation as a bold and methodical commander.
Below: Franco with officers of the Tenerife garrison shortly before the rising.

Right above: (left) The cover of *Ahora* magazine showing Lt José Castillo (on left) and Calvo Sotelo; *(right)* the body of the murdered Calvo Sotelo in the morgue at Madrid.
Right below: Fascist salute of honour at Calvo Sotelo's funeral on 14 July.

LOS EXECRABLES CRIMENES DE AYER.—Primero el teniente de Asalto don José Castillo, y horas más tarde el diputado a Cortes don José Calvo Sotelo, han sido asesinados. Ambos han caído víctimas de los insólitos criminales desatados por el frenesí de la pasión política, a la que el Poder público, como se acuerda en la referencia del Consejo de ministros, tiene que poner inmediatamente un límite infranqueable. En las fotos las dos víctimas, el teniente Castillo y el señor Calvo Sotelo

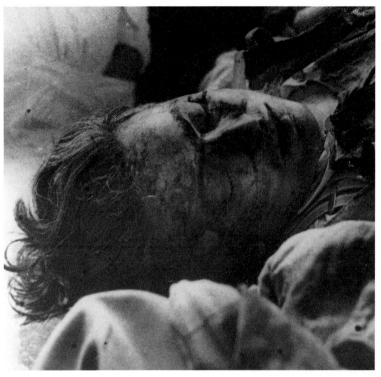

The army rebellion that began in Morocco on 17 July spread quickly to the mainland, where its main initial successes were in the north and centre: *(left)* Pamplona, Navarre, where General Mola *(above)* had the ardent support of Carlist *requetés: (above right)* Vigo in north-western Galicia, which was taken despite a strong working-class movement; *(right)* Vitoria, capital of Alava, which with Navarre went over to the rebels; and *(below)* Segovia, in conservative Old Castile, where the capital Burgos was taken with equal ease.

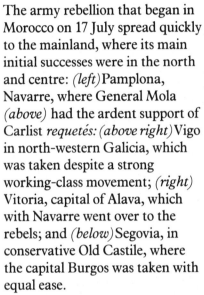

Seville

In the south, Seville was seized for the rebels on 18 July in a daring *coup* by General Queipo de Llano *(left above)*. He took over the radio station and began making the bloodcurdling broadcasts for which he was to become famous — parodied *(left below)* in a French left-wing cartoon of 1937 depicting him as a drunkard. On 20 July, Major Castejón *(below*, with Queipo de Llano) arrived in Seville from Morocco with a few Moroccan troops *(right above)*, flown in by a Fokker aircraft supplied by Hitler in the first airlift in modern warfare. Led by Castejón, they wiped out resistance in the working-class district of Triana with hideous brutality *(right below)*, knifing the men to death in the streets and then demolishing the area by cannon fire.

The Church

The early days of the rising were marked by an explosion of anti-clericalism resulting from popular resentment and suspicion of the Church as the ally of the upper classes. Priests and nuns were massacred indiscriminately and churches sacked. In the propaganda war, the Republican side came to present the Church as the defender of Fascist oppression, while the Nationalists found an ideological anchor in the defence of Catholicism and presented the Civil War as a crusade against the enemies of God.

Left: Desecration of a church in Madrid, by the Nationalist artist Carlos Saenz de Tejada.
Right: 'How the Church has sown its religion in Spain': poster produced in French by the Socialist trades union UGT as part of the international propaganda campaign.
Below: 'The Satisfied Priest', 1936; drawing by the liberal intellectual French artist André Masson.

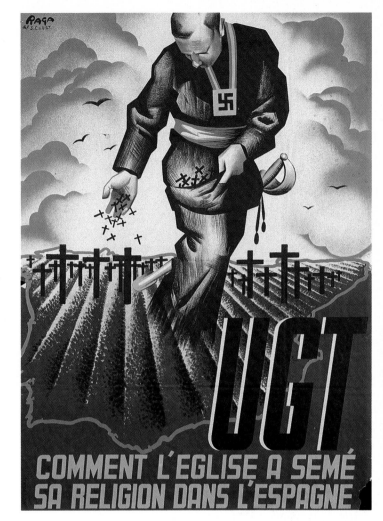

UGT

COMMENT L'ÉGLISE A SEMÉ SA RELIGION DANS L'ESPAGNE

MADRID

In the capital, the unco-ordinated military rising was put down by loyal troops and armed workers after two days of street fighting and mob violence. The Popular Front government vacillated; Prime Minister Casares Quiroga resigned, to be replaced on the night of 19 July, after the fall of the stop-gap government of Martínez Barrio, by the bourgeois Left Republican José Giral. Effective control of the city was in the hands of the Socialist trades union, the UGT. Workers took over the mansions of the wealthy, public buildings, hotels and restaurants, and set up their own street patrols, arresting and searching suspects.

Rebel troops with monarchist and Falangist volunteers took refuge in the Montaña barracks, which was surrounded and stormed by an angry mob on 20 July. On surrender, many of the rebels were shot down in cold blood.

Right: An armed civilian leading away rebel officer prisoners.
Below: Slaughtered rebels in the courtyard of the barracks.

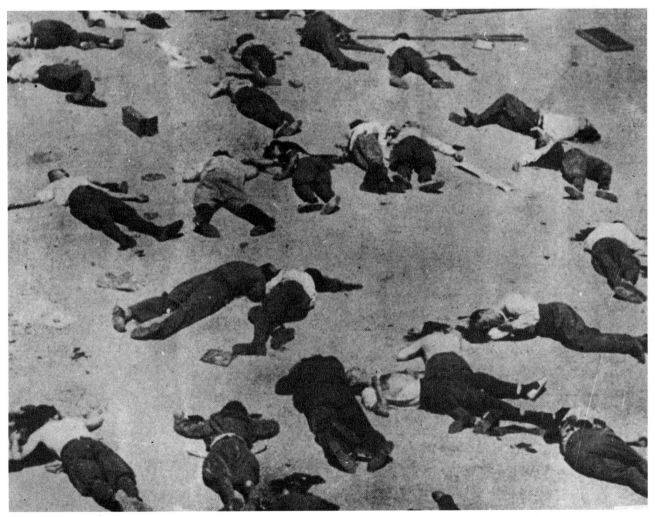

By 22 July General Mola's inexperienced and quite small forces had reached the Guadarrama mountains north of Madrid. The people's militias of the Republican side, hastily formed by workers' committees in response to the rising, were fired by revolutionary fervour and went off for a day's skirmishing in the hills in an atmosphere like a carnival. They were badly equipped and untrained — to the frequent despair of the regular troops among them, who were suspected of disloyalty to the Republic.

Above: Madrid workers leaving for the front, the train daubed with the initials of the main unions responsible for organizing the militias: the Socialist UGT and its rival anarcho-syndicalist union, the CNT/FAI.
Below: Convoy of lorries and requisitioned cars carrying militiamen to the Madrid front on 23 July.
Right: Militiaman and woman at watch on the front in late July.

BARCELONA

The military rebellion in Catalonia's capital was put down after a two-day battle, with the militant workers of the CNT/FAI and the anti-Stalinist POUM joining the loyal Assault and Civil Guards to defeat the rebels. General Goded, arriving from Majorca on the 19th to lead the rising, was captured and later executed. The besieged Atarazanas barracks held out till the 20th, when they were stormed and torn apart. As in Madrid, effective power passed to the people on the streets. President Companys and the Catalan government, the Generalidad, nominally ruled but a dual authority was set up, with real control lying with the Anti-Fascist Militia Committee dominated by the CNT.

Below: Corpses of nuns exposed outside a convent; on 19-20 July, many of the city's churches were desecrated and burnt in outbursts of mob violence that the authorities, official and unofficial, were powerless to control.

Above: Workers manning the street barricades during the fighting on 19-20 July.
Below left: One of the loyal Assault Guards.
Below right: Firing on rebel troops from behind a barricade of horses killed in the fighting.

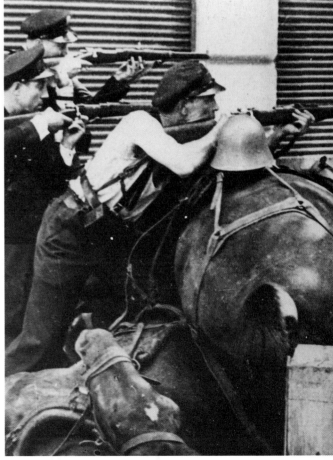

Above: Posters emphasizing the heroic role of the CNT/FAI in fighting the rebels.
Below: 'Map of the Spanish Revolution'.

The Ritz in Barcelona before the war *(below)* and after its revolutionary conversion to a canteen *(above)* by FOSIG, the union in control of the city's hotel and restaurant trade.

Left above: A women's militia unit setting off from Barcelona for the Aragon front; dungarees became the uniform in the early days of the war.

Left below: Lorry requisitioned by the CNT being decked with pictures representing the Republic.

Right: Farewell to a POUM volunteer leaving for Huesca on the Aragon front on 24 July.

Below left: The body of an Assault Guard killed in the Barcelona street fighting, draped with the Catalan flag.

Below right: 'Here fell the first defenders of the Republic at 5.10am on the day of the 19th': note scribbled in Catalan and stuck on a roadside fence.

Pleading for mercy in the village of Constantina, between Seville and Córdoba, captured by Foreign Legion troops on the rebels' march north towards Madrid; August 1936.

3 · The Early Months

1936

August   Fierce battles in mountains to north of Madrid.

August 2   France, after split in Blum Cabinet, announces policy of non-intervention.

August 3   General Castejón launches rebel offensive in Estremadura.

August 6   Franco arrives in Seville to direct campaign from south. In Barcelona, government of Generalidad replaced by Anti-Fascist Militia Committee, dominated by CNT.

August 7   French volunteers enlist for service in Spain. US warns its consuls to observe strict neutrality.

August 8   Republican forces invade Balearic islands, capturing Ibiza and Formentera. First conscriptions in rebel-held zone. France closes border with Spain.

August 10   Indalecio Prieto appeals in radio broadcast for end to Red Terror in Republican zone.

August 12   First International Brigade volunteers arrive in Barcelona. General Goded is executed.

August 14   Legionaries and Moors of General Yagüe's column breach defence at Badajoz; ferocious killings follow. Nationalists now dominate approaches to Portuguese frontier.

August 15   Britain bans export of arms to Spain.

August 16   Republican forces land on Majorca.

August 17   In Asturias, militia units capture last rebel position in Gijón.

August 19   Poet Federico Garciá Lorca executed by Falangists in Granada.

August 22   Modelo prison in Madrid assaulted and political prisoners shot. First British medical convoy leaves for Spain.

August 23   Popular Front tribunals created.

August 24   Marcel Rosenberg, Soviet Union's first ambassador to Spain, takes up post in Madrid. Germany, Italy and Portugal agree 'in principle' to Anglo-French non-intervention proposal.

August 26   Rio Tinto mines occupied by rebel armies.

August 28   First aerial bombardment of Madrid.

September 3   Rebel troops occupy Talavera, last important centre on southern advance to Madrid. Stalin's purge trials begin.

September 4   Republican invasion of Majorca fails. Giral resigns; Largo Caballero becomes Prime Minister of government of Socialists, Communists and Left Republicans.

September 5   General Mola's troops take Irún, cutting off Basque country from France; refugees flee across border.

September 7   José Antonio Aguirre forms autonomous Basque government.

September 9   First meeting of Non-Intervention Committee of European powers in London. Alexander Orlov arrives in Spain to oversee Soviet aid to Republic.

(continued on page 61)

(continued from page 59)

September 13   San Sebastian falls to rebel forces.

September 16   Ronda falls to rebel forces.

September 19   Republican forces ousted from Majorca by Italian Fascist ruler, Conde Rossi.

September 24   CNT joins Generalidad, ending dualistic government in Catalonia.

September 25   In Nationalist (rebel) zone, decree forbids political and trade union activities.

September 27   General Varela's rebel forces take Toledo and relieve siege of Alcazár.

September 29   Franco appointed Head of State as well as Commander in Chief of Nationalist armies. Rebel cruiser *Canarias* sinks Republican destroyer; Republican fleet seeks refuge in Bilbao.

September 30   Republican government creates Popular Army of mixed brigades with military discipline to remedy defects of militias; publishes evidence of German and Italian violation of non-intervention agreement.

Rebels' Advance from the South

Left above: Robert Capa's famous photograph of a Republican volunteer at the instant of death, taken in Andalusia in August 1936 and possibly a posed picture. It was published in France in the autumn of 1936 and later in *Life* magazine, and for many people came to symbolize the war.

Left below: Moroccan troops in the service of the rebels arriving in Spain; the airlift of the Army of Africa under Franco's command began in steady numbers in early August 1936, most of the troops being flown into Seville by Junkers 52.

Right above: Republican planes bombing a bridge near Seville in an unsuccessful attempt to halt the rebels' advance.

Legionaries and Moroccans led by Colonel Yagüe took the frontier town of Badajoz in Estremadura on 14 August, sealing off the Portuguese frontier from the Republicans. An appalling slaughter followed, which produced reprisals in the Republican zone, and was one of the earliest massacres to be reported in the foreign press.

Right centre: Militiaman being led to his execution.

Below: Slaughtered bodies lying in the fields beside the town.

Catalan posters bolstering the revolutionary war effort, 1936.
Left: 'Anti-Fascists! Think of those who are fighting.' Published by the Comintern's International Red Help (SRI).
Right above: 'Workers! Peasants! Unite for victory.'

Right below: Painting by the Nationalist artist A. Kemer of the Simancas barracks in Gijón, which were blown up by Asturian miners on 16/17 August after a heavy resistance; the rebel troops died in the flames. The poor and fiercely Republican port of Gijón was in the control of a committee of CNT, UGT and Communist Party members and during the autumn of 1936 came under constant bombardment from a Nationalist cruiser lying offshore.

Left above: Meeting of the Anti-Fascist Militia Committee, Barcelona, in August 1936. At the end of the table is García Oliver, who is seen with CNT colleagues *(right below)* setting off for a visit to the Aragon front. In November he became Minister of Justice in Largo Caballero's government.

Left below: The Lenin column, made up of volunteers from the anti-Stalinist POUM, lined up in Barcelona ready for the front. Its ranks were joined by George Orwell, who stands head and shoulders above the others in the front row, far left.

Above: POUM demonstration in Barcelona.

Above right: The anarchist leader Federica Montseny addressing a mass meeting in Barcelona, autumn 1936. She agreed to join Largo Caballero's government as Minister of Health at the same time as her fellow-CNT member García Oliver.

Right: Revolutionary propaganda broadcast by newly liberated women in the streets of Barcelona.

Collectivization

In the revolution that took place in the Republican zone, factories, public services, dockyards and commerce were forcibly collectivized to some extent in nearly all the main urban centres; in Catalonia the workers' committees controlled about seventy per cent of industry. There were similar moves to collectivize the land in rural areas, particularly in Aragon, with some villages even abolishing the use of money.

Above: 'Peasants. The land is yours.': poster by POUM, which supported neither the small proprietors protected by the Communists nor the CNT collectives.

Right: Collectivized public transport services, which were under the control of the CNT Transport Union; published in Barcelona.

Aragon Front

Left above: Militiawoman and men in the Aragon hills; probably a posed picture.
Left centre: Shell-damaged kitchen after the fighting at Siétamo, near Huesca, in early August.
Left below: Mixed group of Republican fighters; a few light guns were the average equipment of such a group.
Below: Volunteers of the POUM's ultra-radical youth movement, the JCI, in the Joachín Maurín column.

Above: Grenade-throwers of the Durruti column, the largest and most formidable of the assorted groups fighting on the Aragon front. Their anarchist leader Buenaventura Durruti was a key figure in the Barcelona revolution of the early months; he was killed in Madrid in November 1936.
Right: Protest against the arms kept by the militia in Barcelona to maintain power, while the troops at the front lacked weapons; published in the Catalan magazine *L'Esquella de la torratxa*, 3 September 1936.

Above: Popular tribunal inside Madrid prison. In an attempt to counter the *paseos* — the indiscriminate assassinations of suspected Nationalist sympathizers by 'uncontrollables', popular tribunals were set up in late August 1936 to judge those accused of Fascism. *Below:* Food distribution in Madrid, September 1936. The arrival of refugees fleeing before the Nationalist advance caused an acute food shortage in the capital.

Right: Militiamen surrendering to rebel troops at the Somosierra Pass on the Guadarrama front north of Madrid, August 1936.

Fall of Irún and San Sebastián

After naval and air bombardment followed by fierce fighting on land, General Mola's forces finally took Irún on 4-5 September, effectively cutting off France from the Basque country. A week later the Basque summer resort of San Sebastián surrendered to the Nationalists.

Left above: Nationalist troops in Irún, including a woman wearing a Red Cross armband but carrying weapons.

Left below: Searching for arms in the rebels' mopping-up operations in Irún *(left),* and fighting from a shell-bombed house *(right).*

Above: Refugees arriving by boat on French soil; the smoke on the horizon rises from Irún, parts of which were set alight by anarchists just before the Nationalists entered the town.

Below: Looking across the bay from a shelled hilltop of San Sebastián; the town had come under bombardment from Nationalist warships from 17 August.

Siege of Alcázar

Colonel Moscardó with over a thousand rebel troops and supporters held out in the fortress of Alcázar in Toledo from the start of the rising to 27 September, when they were relieved by Nationalist troops under General Varela. The 'epic' siege became a set-piece of Nationalist propaganda.
Above: The fortress after it had been partly dynamited by Asturian miners on 25 September.
Below: Nationalist troops taking over Toledo.

Above: Archway of the Alcázar from which the rebel inmates fired on the besiegers; painting by the Nationalist artist A. Kemer.
Right: Women survivors of the siege in the cellars where the defenders had lived.

HA MUERTO FRANCO

Según últimas noticias, el general traidor Franco, ha sido muerto por un teniente de la disuelta Guardia Civil.

Las masas populares y antifascistas del pueblo español, conocían sobradamente, la actuación de este canalla traidor.

Como remate a toda una vida de traición y asesinatos, de pueblo, ha muerto como mueren los traidores: Odiado y vilipendiado hasta por sus seguidores en esta sublevación que ensangrienta al pueblo español.

Con su muerte, la unión de todos los antifascistas, se refuerza y la victoria final no se puede hacer esperar.

Milicianos, vuestro valor os hace ser invencibles

Above left: General Franco on his installation as Head of State at Burgos on 1 October 1936. His fellow-generals had voted him Generalissimo 'with all the powers of the Spanish state', on 29 September; *'Dios, Patria, Rey'* — 'One State, One Country, One Chief' — became the Nationalist line.

Above right: On the same day as Franco made his oath of office, the paper of the Socialist youth regiment of 'La Pasionaria' reported his murder by a Civil Guard; many units had their own newspapers.

Below: The funeral of a rebel soldier near Vallodolid.

Right: 'Paseos': a depiction by the Nationalist artist Carlos Sáenz de Tejada of the assassinations by self-appointed vigilante groups that were a feature of the terror in the Republican zone in the early months of the war.

Above: Catalan poster urging people to enlist in the Popular Army, created in the autumn of 1936 to try to control the people's militias and bring efficiency to the Republican forces.
Below left: Barcelona militiamen of the first days of the war.
Below right: Enlistment poster for the President Azaña battalion; militia battalions were incorporated into the new 'mixed brigades'.
Right: Poster of the Iron Column, the most notorious of the anarchist columns and partly made up of ex-convicts. They strongly resisted the threat to their independence from central government.

MADRID 1936

NO PASARAN!

4 · Assault on Madrid and Internationalism

1936

October 1 Basque autonomy approved by Cortes; Aguirre becomes President of Basque 'state', Euzkadi.

October 4 Republican offensive on Oviedo.

October 6 Soviet Union states it will be bound by non-intervention only to same extent as Germany, Italy and Portugal.

October 7 Republican decree confiscates rebel supporters' lands.

October 9 International Brigade members arrive at Alicante.

October 17 Nationalist reinforcements reach Oviedo. Training base for International Brigaders established at Albacete.

October 24 First Russian tanks in action at Aranjuez on Madrid front; German and Italian planes bomb Madrid.

October 31 Hitler decides to provide Franco with airforce of 100 planes.

November 2 Russian fighter planes in action in intensified fighting around Madrid; Nationalists take Brunete.

November 4 Representatives of CNT join Largo Caballero's government.

November 6 Government flees from Madrid to Valencia; General Miaja heads city's defence committee with Colonel Rojo as Chief of Staff.

November 7-23 Assault on Madrid.

November 8-9 Fierce fighting, with first of the International Brigades (XI) in action to help defend University City.

November 15-17 Heavy air and artillery bombardment, with Condor Legion in action; Legionaries and Moors break through to University City; stalemate reached.

November 18 Germany and Italy recognize Franco's Burgos regime.

November 19 Durruti dies in Madrid.

November 20 Falangist leader Primo de Rivera executed in Alicante.

November 23 Frontal attack on Madrid ceases, with lines stabilized.

Opposite: Photomontage of events in Madrid 1936, incorporating the city's famous slogan *'No pasarán'* — 'They shall not pass' — a phrase used by the fiery Communist orator and leader Dolores Ibarruri, 'La Pasionaria' *(above)*.
Below: Republican soldier in Madrid beneath a plaque to Spain's great novelist Pérez Galdos.
Left below: French cartoon published in *Gringoire,* 27 November 1936.

MADRID

FORTIFICACION INEXPUGNABLE

ESTUDIO DE LA COMANDANCIA

UNION POLIGRAFICA. C. O. MADRID.

DEFENSOR

GENERAL MIAJA

Left: Celebratory poster of Madrid's resistance to the Nationalist assault.

Above: Popular tribute to General Miaja, head of the Madrid Defence Committee, who was built up as the city's hero.

Right above: Bomb explosion in Gran Vía; aerial bombardment of Madrid began on 28 August and intensified in November as General Varela's troops closed in on the capital.

Right: Republican troops in action defending University City; a posed picture.

Below: Foreign journalists surveying the Madrid front; the smoke in the distance rises from the bombed capital.

Above: Barricades in the bomb-damaged Calle de Altamirana, near University City in the western quarter of Madrid, where fighting was particularly fierce.
Below: Refugees from the bombing sheltering in Madrid's subway and fleeing with mattresses, their most treasured possession. The City's Defence Committee urged the evacuation of civilians to relieve pressure on food supplies.

Above left: Largo Caballero, the Socialist Prime Minister from September 1936 to May 1937. His government moved from Madrid in November to the safety of Valencia.
Above right: Staff of the British Embassy in Madrid painting a Union Jack on the roof as a signal of 'neutral' territory to raiding aircraft.
Below: The national lottery being held for the first time in Valencia, on 3 December 1936, after the government's move.

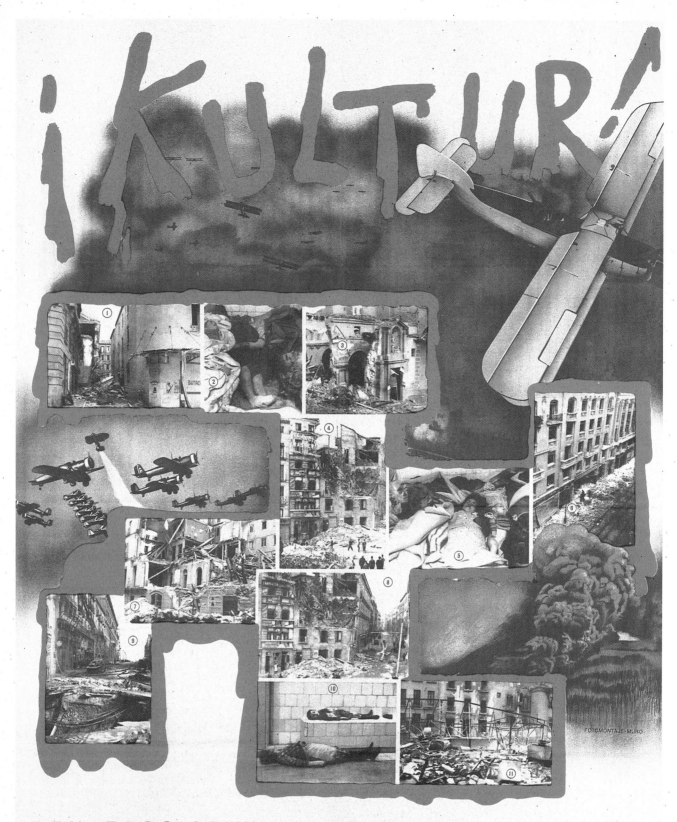

DEN FASCISTIKA BARBARISMEN I MADRID

1) La Plaza de la Opera, efter luft bombardement, med Opera Cinematografen och andra hus — 2) Det ser ut som om de fascistika flygarenas bomber vore riktade främst emot barn! I detta fotografi ses en liten stackare, vars späda kropp blev massakrerad med andra av granat skärvorna — 3) Vad är kvar av San Sebastian kyrkan efter den blev bombarderad av fascisterna, som kalla sig «Katoliker» — 4) Det väl kända Apoteket «Globo» vid Anton Martin gatan efter ett bombardement — 5) Än flere barn, med sina fredliga föräldrar i likhuset — 6) Ett stycke av Calle Mayor och Cine Pleyel — 7) Hus som bombarderats i Leganitos gatan — 8) En vy till av apoteket «Globo» med den store Atocha gatan till höger — 9) Resultatet av ett bombardement i den store Alcala gatan—hörnet av Puerta del Sol (Soltorget) — 10) Fascisterna som vilddjuren förstöra allt. Deras ända objektiv är att döda folk—hälst späda barn! — 11) En del av «Carmen» saluhallarna. förstörda av bombar

C.N.T.   COMITÉ NACIONAL   A.I.T.
(Sección Propaganda)

Non-Intervention

Through the diplomatic efforts of France and Britain, all the European governments signed the non-intervention agreement not to supply arms to Spain. It did not deter Italy and Germany from openly supplying arms and men to the Nationalists or the Soviet Union from sending war material and 'advisors' to the Republic.

Left: Anti-German propaganda featuring photographs of the bombing of Madrid, published by the CNT/FAI in Valencia.

Above: Appeal from the French left to read news of Spain's 'war for liberty and civilisation'.

Below: 'Non-Intervention Poker', by the English cartoonist David Low, published in the French magazine *Vu* in January 1937. The two architects of non-intervention, British Foreign Secretary Anthony Eden (with hands tied behind him) and Léon Blum, Prime Minister of France, sit with Hitler, Mussolini and Stalin.

Soviet Aid

Stalin, in accordance with the non-intervention agreement of the European powers, banned Soviet arms deliveries to Spain at the end of August. Almost simultaneously he ordered the Comintern to assist the Republic to obtain arms and sent a large diplomatic staff to Spain to help administer Soviet aid and to influence events. The Soviet Union became the Republic's primary supplier of war material, for which the Spanish government paid in gold of the the Bank of Spain.

Left: The freighter *Zirianin,* one of the first Soviet ships to bring weapons and food to the Republic, arriving at Barcelona in autumn 1936.

Above: Caricature of Franco, alluding to the arms support of the Fascist German and Italian governments, being paraded through the streets of Moscow during the anniversary celebrations of the Russian Revolution.

Below left: Vladimir Antonov-Ovseyenko, Russian consul-general in Barcelona, at the quayside on the arrival of the *Zirianin* from Odessa; he was a veteran of the Russian Revolution and had commanded the Red Guard unit that stormed the Winter Palace.

Below right: Messages of encouragement from Stalin displayed at a Spanish meeting in homage to the Soviet Union in 1936.

International Brigades

The recruitment drive for the International Brigades, organized by the Comintern from a central office in Paris, began in October 1936. The volunteers were often simply anti-Fascist rather than Communist, and the majority from the working-classes. A base was established in Spain at Albacete, where they were joined by many of the foreign volunteers who had already been in the fighting.

Left above: European volunteers marching through Barcelona on their arrival in October 1936.
Left centre and below: American volunteers: the arrival of the Abraham Lincoln Brigade in Barcelona; Americans enrolling to fight in Spain; and a publication, appealing to America's liberal tradition, to raise money for the battalion.

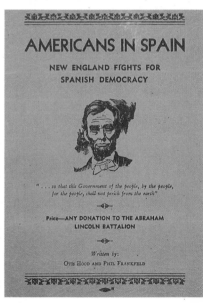

Right: French members of the first International Column, which became the XI Brigade, in Madrid, November 1936. Of some 10,000 French volunteers who fought in the International Brigades, the largest number of any national group, about 3000 were killed.

Below left: André Marty, French commander of the International Brigade base at Albacete and member of the Comintern Executive Committee.

Below right: Luigi Longo, the Italian Communist youth leader who was one of the Comintern's negotiators with Largo Caballero's government to form the International Brigades. He and fellow-Italian Guiseppe di Vittorio were commanders with André Marty of the Albacete base.

British Volunteers

Above left: Volunteer ambulance crew, including the poet Stephen Spender (third from right).
Above: Ambulance supplied by a British aid organization being unloaded at Dieppe.
Left: Women artists who had organized a charity art exhibition to raise money for the ambulance behind them.
Below: Protest march in East London against the British government's non-intervention policy, October 1936.

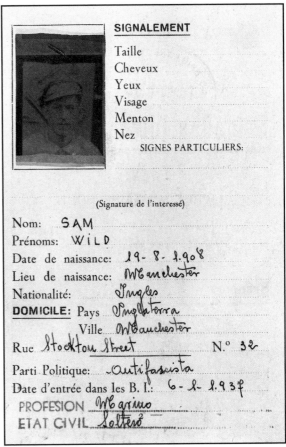

SIGNALEMENT
Taille
Cheveux
Yeux
Visage
Menton
Nez
       SIGNES PARTICULIERS:

(Signature de l'interessé)

Nom: SAM
Prénoms: WILD
Date de naissance: 19-8-1.908
Lieu de naissance: Manchester
Nationalité: Ingles
DOMICILE: Pays Inglaterra
        Ville Manchester
Rue Stockton Street   N.° 32
Parti Politique: Antifascista
Date d'entrée dans les B. I.: 6-1-1.937
PROFESION Marino
ETAT CIVIL Soltero

Above left: Members of the British No 1 Company at Albacete, wearing French World War I uniforms; photographed after returning from the Madrid front in January 1937.

Above right: International Brigade passport of Sam Wild, a Manchester labourer and sailor, who became Commander of the British Battalion and was in action from early 1937 to the return home of the Brigades in late 1938.

Below: British volunteers with a makeshift washing machine at the Aragon front, autumn 1936. Some 170 men and women worked behind the front lines as administrators, mechanics or in the medical service as doctors, nurses and ambulance drivers: Australian, New Zealand and Canadian nurses were a particularly strong element.

94

Posters displayed in the Spanish Republican zone to promote the international aspect of the war.
Left: Appeal to workers' solidarity, published in Valencia, December 1936.
Right above: 'All the peoples of the world are in the International Brigades on the side of the Spanish people.'
Right below: 'The International Brigades at the core of the Popular Army help defend your wealth and homeland.' Both posters were produced by the UGT syndicate of professional artists.

Above: Demonstration in New York in support of the Republic. Roosevelt's government followed the European non-intervention policy throughout the war.
Below: Members of an American medical unit in Tarancón, Cuenca; the woman is the volunteer driver of the ambulance, one of eighteen provided by the American Medical Bureau to Aid Spanish Democracy.

Relief Organizations

Numerous relief organizations to help the Republic were formed in most countries of the world by the autumn of 1936, ranging from local charities knitting garments for refugees to medical aid committees raising money for ambulances, medical personnel and supplies, and appeal organizations such as Friends of Spain.

Right above: Swedish donations of clothing and blankets for the Republic.
Right centre: A Swiss ambulance donated by Friends of the Spanish Republic and the Socialist syndicates, in Barcelona, October 1936. Of the Swiss among the International Brigaders, 76 were killed in the fighting.
Below: Collecting contributions from Parisians in a Spanish Republican flag *(left)*
as part of an appeal campaign from a barge on the Seine carrying food and clothing supplies for Spain *(right)*.

Death of the Falangist Leader

The execution of José Antonio Primo de Rivera by the Republican authorities on 20 November 1936 made him into a Nationalist martyr. For Franco, the death of the respected and popular Falangist leader removed a major threat to his leadership and enabled him to bring the Falangists into line.

Above: José Antonio's body, which was exhumed by the Nationalists at the end of the war, being carried in a 24-hour procession from Alicante to a burial place of honour at El Escorial.
Below: Boys of Franco's Fascist youth organization drill-training in Burgos *(right)* and on a field exercise *(left);* the boy wears a Falangist cap.
Right: Nationalist poster incorporating the Falangist red arrow emblem and proclaiming the fight for 'the fatherland, bread and justice'.

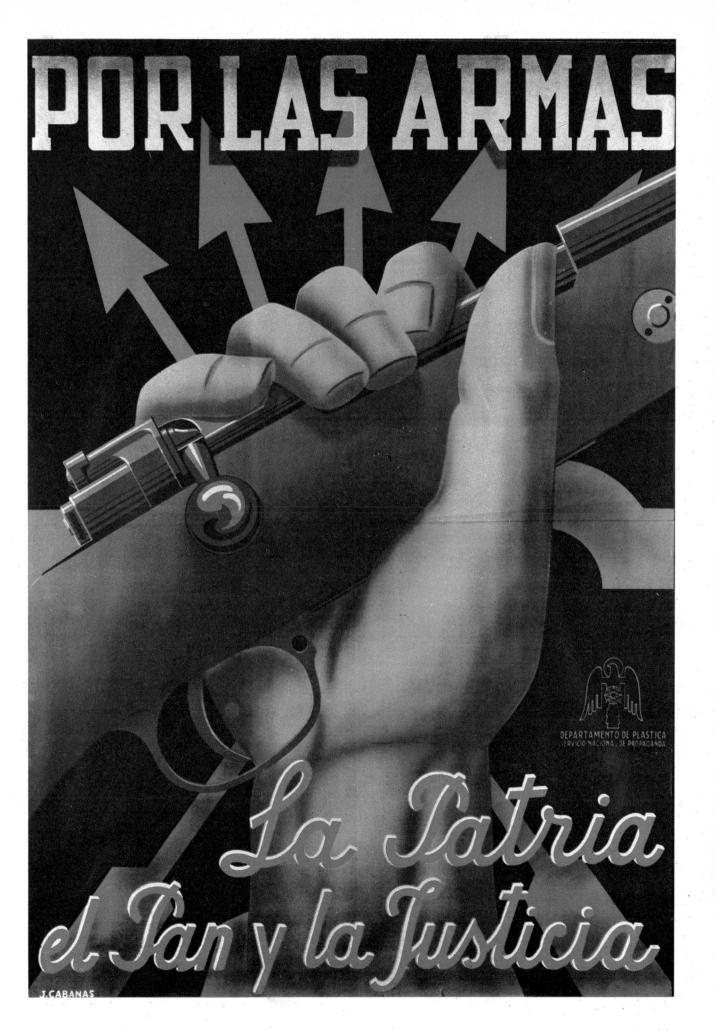

Recognition of Franco's Regime

Germany and Italy, as the 'bulwarks of Western Christian civilization', recognized Franco's regime on 8 November 1936, greeting it as the 'peak of life in the world'.

Left: One of the numerous posters of the caudillo that were put up throughout the Nationalist zone.
Below: The Nationalist headquarters at Burgos, autumn 1936, displaying the alliance with Germany, Italy and Portugal.
Right above: Bishops in Santiago showing their support for Franco; to the right stand General Dávila, member of the Burgos junta, and behind him General Aranda.
Right below: Women of the Spanish nobility saluting the Nationalist flag in Gandesa.

5 · War of Attrition

1936

December   Nationalist attacks around Madrid.

December 6   Port of Barcelona under air attack.

December 14   Nationalist cruiser *Canarias* sinks Soviet supply vessel.

December 17   POUM ousted from Generalidad at Communist insistence.

December 22-23   First Italian Blackshirt 'volunteer' units arrive in Cádiz.

December 23   CNT-dominated Council of Aragon recognized by central government.

1937

January 2   British Foreign Secretary Anthony Eden makes 'gentleman's agreement' with Italy to maintain status quo in Mediterranean.

January 3-17   Nationalist attacks on western Madrid front; government orders evacuation of civilians; fighting ends inconclusively.

January 6   US passes law to forbid export of arms to Spain, reinforcing previous 'moral embargo'.

January 13   Nationalist offensive begins around Málaga with Italian aid.

January 17   Marbella taken by Nationalists.

February 5-24   Battle of Jarama, on south-eastern Madrid front; first participation of Abraham Lincoln Brigade; ends in stalemate after heavy casualties.

February 7-8   Málaga taken by Nationalists with help of Italian troops; refugees flee towards Almería under heavy bombing.

February 14   Mass demonstration of POUM and FAI in Barcelona against government's emphasis on war victory over social revolution.

February 20   Non-Intervention Committee forbids enlistment of volunteers to serve in Spain.

February 21   Largo Caballero dismisses General Asensio, Undersecretary of War, under Communist pressure and sacks Communist staff in return. Strong attacks on Largo Caballero in Communist press follow.

March 8-18   Battle of Guadalajara, with Italian troops in vanguard of Nationalist offensive on north-eastern Madrid front; clash with Italians of Garibaldi Brigade (10th); successful Republican counter-attack (18th), taking Brihuega; Madrid stalemate to continue for next two years.

March 26   Crisis in Generalidad over anarchist objections to conscription to People's Army.

March 30   General Mola begins Nationalist offensive on northern front, in Basque province of Vizcaya; Condor Legion bombs Durango.

Italian troops at Guadalajara, March 1937.

Nationalist Troops at the Madrid Front

Above: Mass celebrated in the Guadarrama hills, 6 January 1937.

Left: Injured troops, mostly Moroccan, returning from the fighting.

Below left: Sitting out the winter in a trench outside Madrid.

Below right: Reinforcements arriving at Talavera station.

Battle of Jarama

Intense fighting around the River Jarama south-east of Madrid continued for most of February, in awful weather and with heavy losses to both sides. The Republican and International Brigade troops with Russian tanks and air support finally stemmed the Nationalist offensive, which threatened to cut the Madrid-Valencia highway.

Above: American volunteers, many of them students, arriving at Le Havre en route to Spain, January 1937. They were thrown into the battle on 23 February, when over half the men were killed on their first day of fighting.

Below: British of the XV Brigade hauling an anti-tank gun. They held 'Suicide Hill' on the night of 12 February at great cost; the grave *(right)* commemorated the 375 dead out of 600.

Fall of Málaga

Italian Blackshirts under General Roatta moved on Málaga in January 1937, while Nationalist forces directed by General Queipo de Llano closed in from the west, taking Marbella, and from Granada to the north-east. The Republican town, isolated from any support from the north, was entered by the Italians on 8 February after heavy air and sea bombardment. Refugees fled along the coast road to Almería under constant shelling.

Above: Italian pro-Nationalist painting of troops in action at Málaga; about 5000 Blackshirts were involved in the town's capture.
Below: Italian tanks in the town centre.

Above left: Postcard published in Rome proclaiming that the Italian Blackshirts would crush the brutal forces of the left in Spain.

Above right: Women making the Fascist salute after Málaga's occupation.

Below: Nationalist propaganda postcard showing Franco's allegiance with Hitler and Mussolini, sent to England from Málaga in July 1937.

Battle of Guadalajara, 8-18 March

The struggle for the town of Guadalajara north-east of Madrid took place in driving rain, with Italian troops leading the Nationalist offensive. After bitter fighting in which many of the Italians were killed or captured, the government forces held their position.

Left above: The Guadalajara front, a shell exploding in the background.
Left below: One of the many dead on the muddy battlefield.
Below left: Front of the XIIth Brigade newspaper, 2 April; this Brigade included the Garibaldi battalion, which confronted fellow-Italians of the Black Flames division.
Below right: French cartoon mocking the Italian defeat, published in an English-language International Brigade paper.
Bottom: Italian prisoners taken at Guadalajara.

THE ROMAN STEP
— Too bad they did not know it at Guadalajara!

"L'Œuvre"

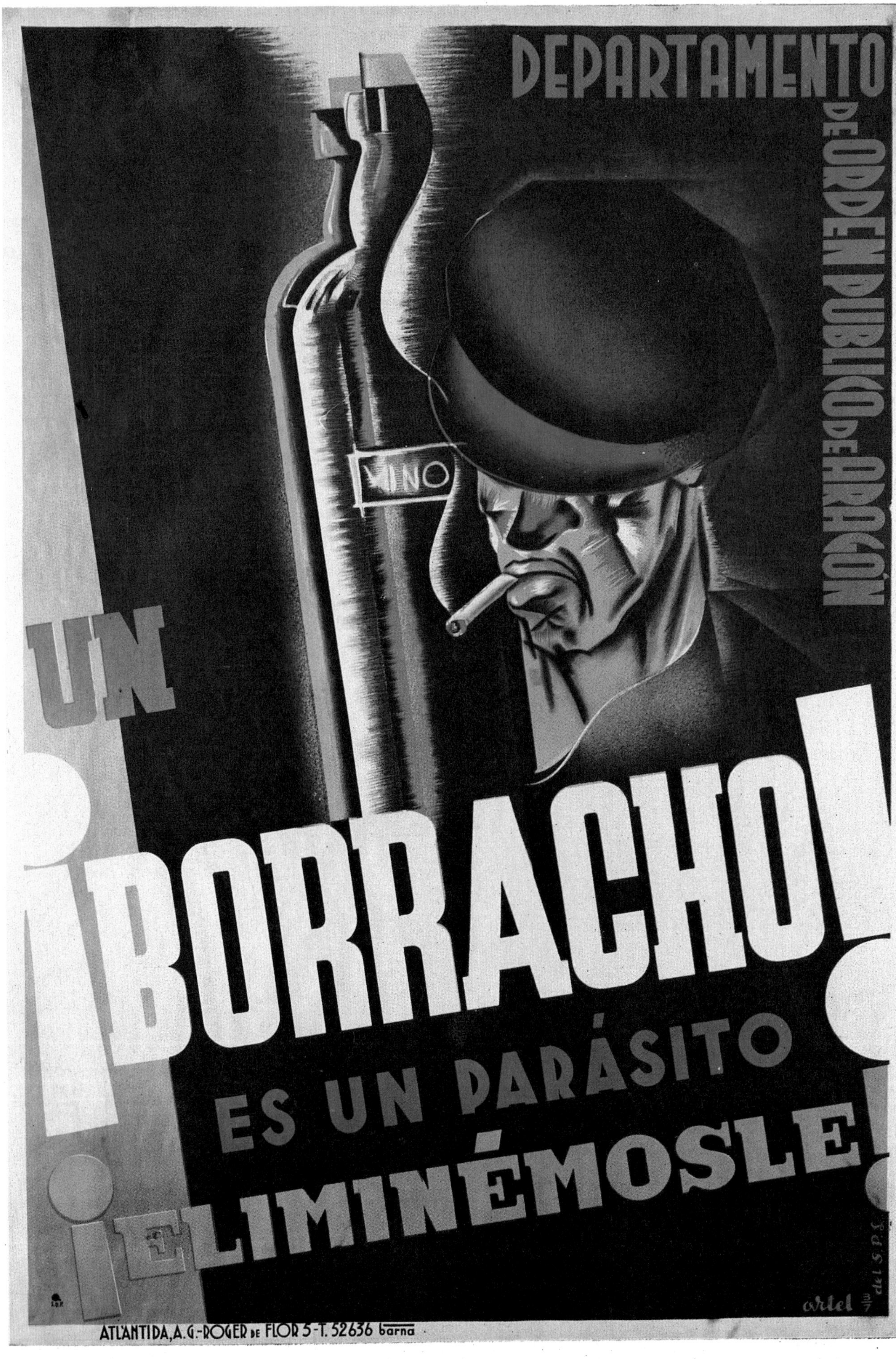
DEPARTAMENTO DE ORDEN PUBLICO DE ARAGÓN
VINO
UN
¡BORRACHO!
ES UN PARÁSITO
¡ELIMINÉMOSLE!
artel
ATLANTIDA, A.G.-ROGER DE FLOR 5-T. 52636 barna

Army Health Campaign

Drunkenness, venereal disease and lice were common problems at the front, which Republican propaganda attempted to counteract.

Above: Republican soldiers at the Madrid front having a makeshift wash.

Right: Posters produced by the Army Health Department, Valencia. *(Above)* 'Soldier, wash yourself. Cleanliness keeps you healthy.' *(Below)* 'Venereal diseases threaten your health. Protect yourself from them.'

Left: 'A drunk is a parasite. Eliminate him.' Published in Barcelona by the Aragon Department of Public Order.

Below: Beer wagon serving the Popular Army.

Behind the Lines

Left: Clothes and equipment for the Popular Army being produced and packaged in the workshops of Barcelona.

Right: Children's ward of a Barcelona hospital *(above)* and a girl refugee awaiting departure *(below)*.

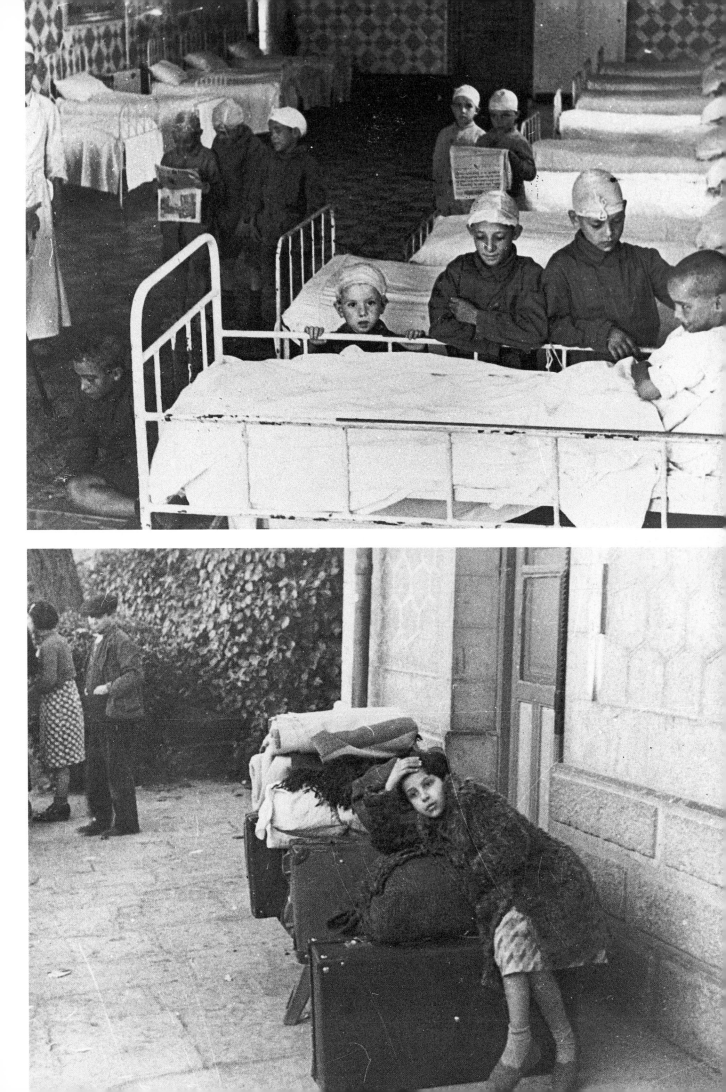

6 · The Basque Country and May Events in Barcelona

1937

April   Offensive in Basque country.

April 18   Franco's Decree of Unification amalgamates Falange and Carlist movements in a single party under his leadership. After internal warfare among Falangists at meeting in Salamanca, leader Manuel Hedilla arrested and later sentenced to death.

April 19   Non-Intervention Committee establishes short-lived land and sea patrol.

April 26   Guernica destroyed in bombing by Condor Legion.

May 3-7   Mini civil war in Barcelona as anarchists and POUM confront Communists and Generalidad security forces; revolutionary forces in Barcelona and Catalan independence of central government destroyed; General Pozas sent to command army of Catalonia.

May 16   Largo Caballero forced to resign after opposition by Communist ministers and their allies to his military offensive in Estremadura and his clemency towards POUM.

May 17   Dr Juan Negrín becomes Prime Minister of new Communist government.

May 29   German cruiser *Deutschland* attacked by Republican planes at Ibiza.

May 31   German fleet bombards Almería in reprisal; Germany and Italy withdraw from Non-Intervention Committee's sea patrol agreement.

June   Offensive in Basque country continues.

June 3   General Mola is killed in air crash on way to consult with General Varela.

June 12   Nationalists break through Bilbao's 'ring of steel'.

June 16   POUM is outlawed and its leaders arrested; Andrés Nin dies in prison (21st) after torture by Soviet agents.

June 19   Nationalist forces enter Bilbao; refugees throng harbour to escape by ship.

June 21   Blum ministry resigns; succeeded by Chautemps.

June 26   Nationalists take Santander.

June 30   Portugal withdraws from Non-Intervention Committee's sea patrol agreement.

Above: Poster decrying the Condor Legion bombing of the Basque country town of Durango on 31 March. Several nuns and priests were killed by direct hits on churches, which had particular significance in the Basque provinces where religion continued to be important.

Left: Catalan appeal to help Euzkadi. Catalonia looked with sympathy on its fellow separatists and this propaganda poster for the creation of a Regular Army combines the Basque and Catalan flags.

115

The Bombing of Guernica

On 26 April, the Condor Legion destroyed the market town of Guernica, ancient capital of the Basques, in a series of air strikes that culminated in incendiary bombing. Some 1600 people were killed and 900 injured, and the town was reduced to rubble. The event would not compare with Allied and German bombings of the Second World War but as the first saturation bombing of a defenceless town to capture attention, it created an international scandal, outraging people of both the politically right and left. The Nationalist press tried to disclaim responsibility by announcing that Guernica had been destroyed by retreating 'reds'.

Above: Condor Legion pilot at the cockpit controls.
Below: Guernica in flames.

Above: Visiting the town after its destruction, the trees blasted bare.
Below: Homeless victims of the bombing.

Pablo Picasso's *Guernica* expressed the horrors of war and the universal outrage at the destruction of the Basque town *(above* and, with the artist beneath it, *left)*. It was first exhibited in Paris in 1937 and became the most famous painting of the war. Picasso had lived outside Spain since 1903 but remained deeply sympathetic to the left cause; like many other well-known artists, he contributed work free.

Below: Picasso drawing used for the jacket of an American left-wing booklet.

Right: French anti-Fascist leaflet of 1937 by the Spanish artist Joan Miró, who was resident in Paris.

SPAIN AND PEACE
By HOWARD FAST

Dans la lutte actuelle, je vois du côté fasciste les forces
périmées, de l'autre côté le peuple dont les immenses ressources
créatrices donneront à l'Espagne un élan qui étonnera
le monde.   Miró.

The Condor Legion

The pictures here are from film believed to have been taken in Spain and found in Germany by the Americans during World War II. The air squadron's commander and director of the Guernica operation, General von Richthofen, appears in the picture top left (seated).

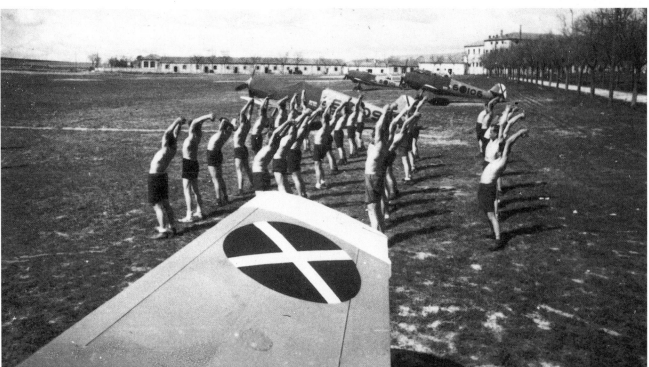

May Events in Barcelona

Open fighting broke out on 3 May between the POUM and anarchist groups intent on pursuing the revolution and the Communists and Catalan government with their emphasis on winning the war. After four days of confusion in which about 500 people were killed and 1000 wounded, order was restored, ensured by the presence of Assault Guards dispatched from Valencia. The mini civil war marked the end of the Catalan revolution and was followed by the fall of Largo Caballero under Communist pressure and a witch-hunt of the POUM and other anti-Stalinist Marxists.

Above: Catalan government troops fighting at the barricades in front of the church of San Jaime.
Right above: POUM poster of April 1937 demanding the creation of a workers' government to replace the Generalidad, which included bourgeois elements; other demands include the forming of a workers' army and

LA SOLUCIÓ DE LA CRISI
QUE PROPOSA EL
P. O. U. M.

RESOLUCIO DEL COMITE CENTRAL DEL P.O.U.M. DAVANT LA CRISI DEL GOVERN DE LA GENERALITAT

«La crisi plantejada en el Govern de la Generalitat de Catalunya, 'atent des del moment de la seva constitució, és una crisi de poder. No hi ha en efecte a Catalunya un Govern capaç de fer complir els seus decrets i disposicions. I aquest Govern no existeix perquè els que s'han constituït fins a la data no són un reflex de la situació creada després del 19 de juliol. Aquesta situació es caracteritza pel paper actiu exercit per les masses treballadores, tant en la lluita armada contra el feixisme com en l'obra de reconstrucció econòmica i política del país sobre noves bases. Manca un Govern que canalitzi les aspiracions d'aquestes masses donant una solució radical i concreta a tots els problemes mitjançant la creació d'un ordre nou que sigui la garantia de la revolució i de la victòria al front de batalla. Aquest Govern no pot ésser altre que un govern format per representants de totes les organitzacions polítiques i sindicals de la classe treballadora, que es proposi com a fi immediat la realització del següent programa :

1er. Socialització de la gran indústria i del transport.
2on. Nacionalització de la Banca.
3er. Municipalització de l'estatge.
4rt. Formació d'un Exèrcit controlat per la classe treballadora.
5è. Constitució d'un Cos de Seguretat Interior únic, a base de les Patrulles de Control i del Cos d'Investigació creats per la revolució i amb la incorporació dels individus dels antics Cossos que hagin demostrat llur fidelitat a la classe obrera.
6è. Ofensiva immediata a Aragó.
7è. Reducció dels grans sous.
8è. Monopoli del comerç exterior.
9è. Creació d'una potent indústria de guerra socialitzada i rigorosament centralitzada.
10. Nacionalització de la terra, que ha d'ésser lliurada en usdefruit als qui la treballen, als quals seran concedits els crèdits necessaris. Explotació col·lectiva de les grans hisendes i auxili econòmic a aquelles explotacions de tipus col·lectiu creades en el curs de la revolució i que hagin demostrat llur vitalitat.
11. Lluita implacable contra els acaparadors i agiotistes per mitjà d'un control rigorós i directe de la distribució i els preus de les subsistències.
12. Organització ràpida i eficient de la defensa aèria i marítima de tot el territori.
13. Convocatòria d'un congrès de delegats dels sindicats obrers i camperols i dels combatents, que estableixi les bases fonamentals del nou règim i elegeixi un Govern obrer i camperol que serà el més democràtic que s'hagi conegut per tal com expressarà inequívocament la voluntat de la immensa majoria del país i tindrà tota l'autoritat per a afiançar el nou ordre revolucionari.»

abril 1937
Barcelona

the nationalization of land and banks.
Right: Andrés Nin, the POUM's leading figure and a former secretary of Trotsky, though no longer in agreement with him. In June the POUM was outlawed and Nin was arrested and murdered by Soviet agents.

Left: Ambulance unit on an otherwise deserted street taking away casualties of the May events in Barcelona.
Left below: Assault Guards parading through the streets of Barcelona on 11 May to signify the restoration of order; and *(below)* the armoured cars that they used.
Bottom: Barricade in front of the headquarters of the CNT Building Industry Syndicate; and *(right above)* women taking down a barricade on 7 May.
Right below: (Left) Publication of 20 May announcing the newly formed government of Dr Negrín and proclaiming its Popular Front policies as the only way to win the war. *(Centre)* Indalecio Prieto, the 'moderate' Socialist who joined with the Communists to overthrow Largo Caballero. He became Minister of Defence in Negrín's new government of 17 May. *(Right)* Cartoon of Franco having been driven to suicide by the 'embrace of the workers'; from a comic paper sympathetic to the revolution and to Largo Caballero, published after the May events.

Left: Carlos Sáenz de Tejada, the best known of the Nationalist artists, at work in his studio using a soldier as a model. His depictions of war scenes are in marked contrast to the representations of workers and fighters in Republican posters.

Above: Sáenz de Tejada's impression of Bilbao's 'ring of iron', the supposedly strong chain of defence around the city.

Fall of Bilbao

Nationalist troops under General Dávila broke
through the 'ring of iron' on 12 June. A mass
civilian evacuation of the city followed and on 19
June Bilbao fell without a battle, leaving its
valuable iron-works and nearby mines intact.
Left above: Nationalist troops and armoured
vehicles in Bilbao the day after its occupation.
Left below: Victory mass held outside San Nicolás
church.
Above: Bilbao harbour, which came under shelling
just before the city's fall.
Right: One of the 3500 child refugees brought
from Bilbao to a camp near Southampton,
England, through funds raised by various
charitable and left-wing organizations.

AMERICAN DEMOCRACY
vs. THE
SPANISH HIERARCHY

Above: Booklet published by the American Committee to Aid Spanish Democracy, part of the pamphlet war over the Spanish bishops' joint letter of 1 July 1937 supporting the Nationalist cause.
Opposite: Republican propaganda caricaturing the elements of the Burgos junta: bishop, general, Nazi capitalist and Moors, sailing from Lisbon with weapons of destruction; the gallows-mast is labelled with Franco's cry 'Spain Arise'.

7 · Steady Nationalist Advance

1937

July 1   Spanish bishops endorse Franco regime in collective letter.

July 6-26   Popular Army offensive on western Madrid front to relieve Northern front; Brunete captured (6th) and retaken by Nationalists by 26th; considerable air fighting and heavy casualties.

July 28   Generalidad reorganized to exclude anarchists.

August 7   Private religious ceremonies re-permitted in Republican zone.

August 10   Anarchist-dominated Council of Aragon dissolved and its powers taken over by Negrín government; de-collectivization follows.

August 15   Republic creates SIM (Servicio de Investigacíon Militar); intensification of political police terror.

August 24   Popular Army begins offensive on Aragon front; battle of Belchite to continue into October.

August 26   Nationalist and Italian troops take Santander. Attacks from unknown sources begin on neutral ships making for Republican ports.

August 28   Vatican formally·recognizes Franco's regime.

September 1   Nationalists begin offensive in Asturias.

September 6   Republican forces finally take Belchite.

September 10   Nyon Conference of main European powers convenes to discuss recent shipping attacks; agreement to institute naval and air patrols.

September 24   Italian Blue Arrows begin counter-offensive at Belchite.

October 1   Largo Caballero removed from executive of Socialist party.

October 6   Nationalist launch counter-offensive in Aragon.

October 17   Largo Caballero publicly attacks Negrín's conduct of the war.

October 19   Gijón finally falls to Nationalists in Asturias offensive, followed by Avilés and Oviedo, completing Nationalist capture of the north.

October 29   Republican government moves from Valencia to Barcelona.

November 6   Italy joins German-Japanese anti-Comintern pact.

November 12   CNT withdraws representatives from Popular Front Committees.

November 17   Britain's Lord Halifax visits Hitler.

November 28   Franco begins naval blockade of Spanish coast.

Battle of Brunete, 6-26 July

The Republican attack around Brunete, west of Madrid, bogged down in confusion after initial success. The Nationalists were able to bring in reinforcements, including the Condor Legion from the north, and successfully counter-attacked on 18 July. After desperate resistance, the Republicans were left with a minute territorial gain and about 25,000 men dead.

Left above: Bombing of the Brunete road.

Left inset: Juan Modesto *(left)*, commander of the Vth Army Corps, and Enriqué Lister, head of its 11th Division, which opened the Brunete attack. Modesto, a former woodcutter, and Lister, a former quarryman, were seasoned Communists and among the best trained commanders of the Republican army.

Left below: Offensive at Villanueva de la Cañada, to north of Brunete, directed by El Campesino of the Vth Corps' 46th Division.

Above: Casualty being carried from the Brunete battlefield.

Below: Recovering from injuries at an American hospital behind the lines *(left)* and *(right)* an operating room; the Civil War was the first war in which casualty figures were considerably reduced as a result of modern anaesthetics and antibiotics.

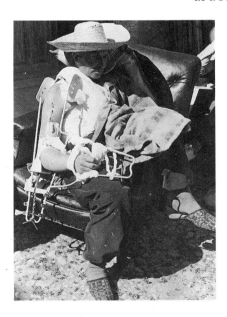
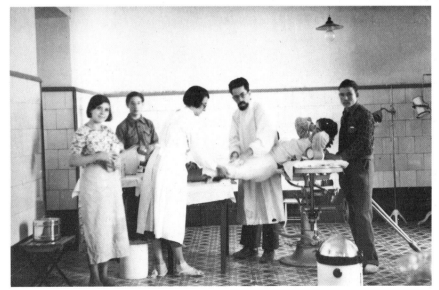

Literacy and Education

A consistent campaign was carried out in the Republican zone to combat widespread illiteracy and to create an educated army and public. *Right:* 'Illiteracy blinds the spirit. Study, soldier.' *Left:* Posters calling for workers to read the anarchist CNT newspaper *Solidaridad (above)* and the Socialist morning paper *Adelante (below)*. *Below:* Soldier reading the Republican version of the daily newspaper *ABC*, formerly a monarchist paper. The CNT had taken over its Madrid offices at the start of the war and continued to publish it from there, while the Nationalists published their version of *ABC* from Seville.

Life at the Front

Above: Lesson in trench building for Republican soldiers, run by the Cultural Militias set up early in the war to create an informed — and it was hoped revolutionary — working-class culture.
Below left: British International Brigaders, including professional musician George Green (playing cello), in a scratch quintet with Spanish workers; the guitarist is the village plumber.
Below right: Militiaman getting help with the tough new leather leggings issued to Republican troops.
Right: Spanish kitchen staff at the monastery hospital at Huete, south-east of Madrid, run by international volunteers.

Right: English-language brochure published in 1938 by Franco's newly established Tourist Department advertising a touring holiday through the conquered towns of the north; Nationalist propaganda showing confidence of ultimate victory to an international audience.

Fall of the North

After the fall of the Basque provinces, the Nationalists moved on Santander and Asturias. The surrender of the city of Santander on 26 August was followed by the fall of Gijón and Oviedo in October, completing the capture of the north and giving Franco control of the Asturian coal mines.

Left above: Carlist troops marching through Santander.
Left centre: Quayside at Santander where Basques who had retreated west were now being evacuated.
Above: Bomb destruction in Oviedo, the chief Asturian city.

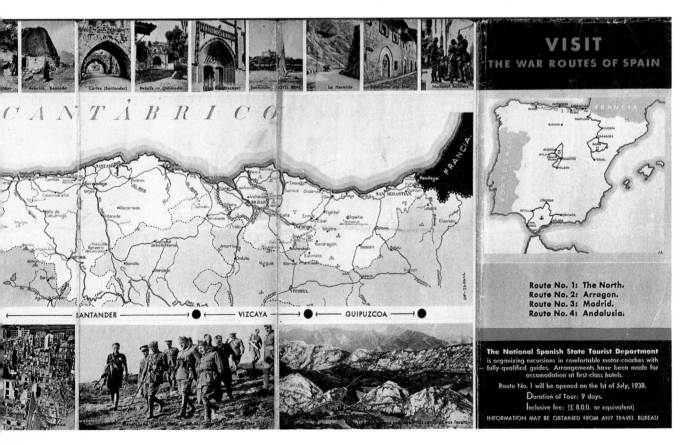

VISIT
THE WAR ROUTES OF SPAIN

Route No. 1: The North.
Route No. 2: Arragon.
Route No. 3: Madrid.
Route No. 4: Andalusia.

The National Spanish State Tourist Department
is organizing excursions in comfortable motor-coaches with fully-qualified guides. Arrangements have been made for accomodation at first-class hotels.

Route No. 1 will be opened on the 1st of July, 1938.

Duration of Tour: 9 days.

Inclusive fee: (£ 8.0.0. or equivalent)

INFORMATION MAY BE OBTAINED FROM ANY TRAVEL BUREAU

Aragon Offensive, August–October 1937

After prolonged and fierce fighting, the Republican attack against the Nationalist line around Huesca, Saragossa and Belchite ended with minimal Republican gains and heavy casualties.

Left above: Republican troops and war correspondents, including the Catalan photographer Agusti Centelles *(centre)*, in Belchite before its recapture by the Nationalists.
Left below: Artillery unit of the Popular Army in the hills by Saragossa.
Above left: Assault Guards firing from a barricade during the siege of Belchite.
Above right: Cigarette and drink supplies for Nationalist troops in recaptured Belchite.
Below: Machine-gun unit of the Abraham Lincoln battalion on the Aragon front; the XVth Brigade played a major part in the battles, during which the Americans' commander, Captain Thompson, was killed.

RECOGER TODA la COSECHA SIGNIFICA DAR A NUESTRO EJERCITO LO QUE NECESITA PARA SOSTENER la LUCHA

MINISTERIO DE AGRICULTURA
INSTITUTO DE REFORMA AGRARIA

Food Production Campaign

Faced by serious food shortages, the Republican government encouraged small peasant proprietors to increase production and tried to prevent sales through the flourishing black market. Shortage of labour largely due to peasants fighting in the army made it difficult to bring in the harvest, commonly done by primitive farming methods *(above)*.

Left: 'Reaping the harvest means giving our army what it needs to continue the fight'; published by the Ministry of Agriculture in Valencia.
Below left: Appeal to peasants not to sell their produce on the free (black) market but through the government co-operatives.
Below centre: 'Defend small property. Capital punishment for thieves.'
Below right: 'To intensify production is to work for the revolution'; published in Barcelona during the Catalan 'battle of the eggs' campaign.

Nyon Conference

In September, the British called a conference to discuss recent attacks on ships in the Mediterranean by 'unknown' submarines. Italy, known to be responsible, and Germany did not attend. The British and French agreed to set up Mediterranean patrols and the attacks temporarily ceased.

Above: Delegates at a banquet during the conference: French Foreign Minister Yvon Delbos (foreground, centre) is opposite British Foreign Secretary Anthony Eden (with cigar) and (left, hand to head) Russian minister Maximo Litvinov.

Left above: Demonstration in London against the appeasement policy towards Italy and Germany of Prime Minister Neville Chamberlain.

Left: Cartoons from an International Brigade paper depicting Mussolini and Hitler as 'unknown' submarines *(left)* and Mussolini *(right)* pondering 'Nyon? Perhaps that's the name of a merchant ship we have not yet sunk'.

144

Above: Members of the Republic's government visiting the Madrid front in November 1937: (from left) Foreign Minister José Giral, Prime Minister Juan Negrín and President Azaña accompanied by General Miaja.

Below: British Labour Party leader Clement Attlee (with pipe) and Labour leaders Ellen Wilkinson (in hat, behind him) and Philip Noël-Baker in Madrid during a visit to the Republic and International Brigaders in late 1937. After the visit, the British contingent was known as the Major Attlee Company.

8 · Republican Defeats

1937

December 8   Nationalists air-bomb Barcelona; Republicans air-bomb León.

December 15   Popular Army begins offensive on Teruel planned by General Rojo and War Minister Prieto.

December 22   Most of Teruel captured by Republican forces.

December 24   Nationalist counter-offensive, with Condor Legion support, begins on Teruel front.

1938

January 8   Last Nationalist resistance overcome in Teruel.

January 30   Franco forms his first ministry.

February 1   Cortes convenes at monastery of Montserrat.

February 5-9   Nationalist offensive along Alfambra River on Teruel front under Franco; cavalry action and heavy air bombardment; ends in Republican defeat.

February 20   Anthony Eden resigns as Foreign Secretary in protest at Chamberlain seeking agreement with Italy before settlement of Spanish question.

February 22   Teruel recaptured by Nationalists.

March 5-6   Nationalist cruiser *Baleares* sunk by Republican destroyers.

March 9   Franco's government issues Labour Charter proposing corporate organization of Nationalist Spain through 'vertical syndicates'; strikes made treasonable; many reforms promised (few of which to be effected).

March 10   Nationalists launch offensive in Aragon aiming to reach river Ebro and the sea, thus cutting Republican zone in two.

March 11   Hitler's armies occupy Austria.

March 12   Franco's government repeals Republic's civil marriage law.

March 13   Blum forms his second Popular Front government; Negrín flies to Paris to plead for re-opening of border.

March 16-18   Round-the-clock bombing of Barcelona by Italian planes based in Majorca.

March 17   France opens border with Spain.

March 22   After taking Caspe, Nationalists move towards sea.

March 28   Indalecio Prieto calls for peace negotiations to begin immediately.

(continued on page 154)

Nationalist troops on the bleak Teruel front, winter 1937/38.

Battle of Teruel, December 1937 — February 1938

A series of attacks and counter-attacks in and around Teruel on the southern Aragon front ended in disastrous defeat for the Republican army, with over 20,000 dead and many more wounded and taken prisoner. Men of both sides suffered from frostbite in temperatures that dropped to as low as 18 degrees below zero.

Above: Republican tanks in Teruel.
Below left: Republican soldier posing beneath a signpost for Teruel.
Below right: Lincoln Brigaders' trench at 'North Pole'; the International Brigades had been resting but were flung into the battle on 19 January after a new Nationalist offensive on the town.

Above: General Yagüe, one of the commanders of the successful Nationalist counter-offensive *(left)* and Carlist troops leaving Teruel after its conquest *(right)*.
Right: Fighting in the bull-ring at Teruel.
Below: Medical unit en route to Teruel; the ambulance was funded by the Canadian Communist Party.

Children's Week

In both the Republican and Nationalist zones, books and toys connected with the war were produced for children. In Barcelona, 1-7 January 1938 was proclaimed the week of the child and advertised throughout the city (*left*, and in a poster by the International Anti-Fascist Solidarity organization, *above left*).

Above right: Children's Sunday comic, *Sidrin*, promoting the Republican war effort.

Right above: A mini-book published to celebrate the 20th anniversary of the Russian revolution *(left)* and a Republican board game *(right)*.

Right: Cut-out Falangist doll with Nationalist uniforms to dress it in.

Hoy es la fiesta de Octubre: hoy se cumplen veinte años que los obreros de Rusia de los burgueses triunfaron.

151

Bombing of Barcelona, March 1938

Left above: Aerial view of bombs being dropped by Nationalist planes on the dock area.

Left centre and below: Wreckage in the city; the child unearthed from the rubble by a rescue team was one of about 1300 people killed and 2000 injured.

Right above: Funeral procession for the victims of the March bombings.

Right below: Shoring up the glass of a chemist's shopfront, the walls alongside plastered with posters.

(continued from page 147)

1938

April 3 General Yagüe's Moroccan forces take Lérida. Blum government falls; succeeded by Daladier ministry which shortly closes border with Spain.

April 4 General Aranda reaches Morella, old Carlist capital.

April 5 Negrín dismisses Prieto under Communist pressure and takes over War Ministry.

April 7 Nationalists take Tremp on the Ebro, which supplied much of Barcelona's electricity.

April 13 General Rojo reports 'total moral crisis' in Republican armies; International Brigades severely depleted in fighting on Ebro front.

April 15 Navarrese units of Nationalist army reach Vinaroz on Mediterranean coast, severing land communication between Valencia and Barcelona.

April 16 Britain makes sweeping naval agreement with Italy; Italy to withdraw troops from Spain on Nationalist victory.

April 20 Nationalist armies reach French border after capturing Aran Valley.

April 21 Nationalist offensive on Valencia begins.

May 1 Negrín announces 13-point programme of Republic's war aims; no shift in attitude of Western democracies results; Franco continues to demand unconditional surrender.

May 3 Franco's government re-establishes Jesuit order.

May 13 Spanish delegate to League of Nations pleads an end to non-intervention policy.

June 13 Nationalists take port of Castellón north of Valencia

Right: Woman distraught beside her dead child, killed in the bombing of Lérida.

Above: Republican troops crossing into France, in flight from the advancing Nationalist armies, April 1938.

Left: One of Prime Minister Negrín's 13 Proposals of 1 May guaranteeing freedom of conscience and religion.

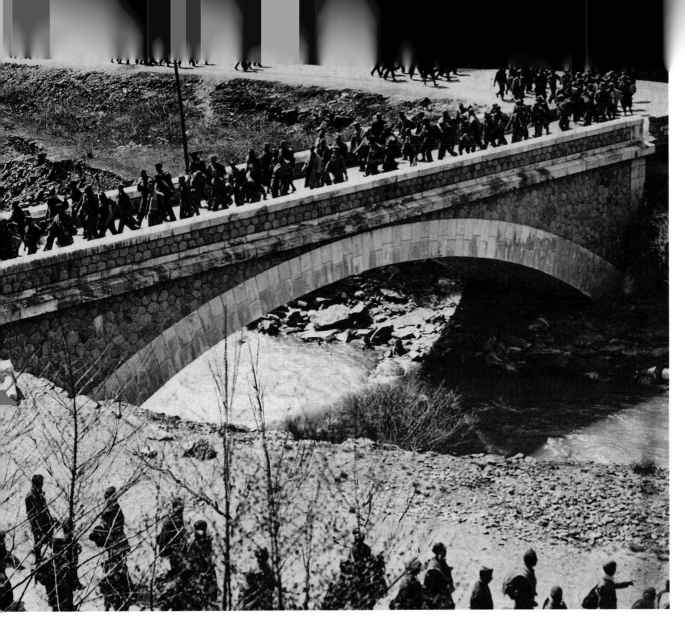

Right: British right-wing propaganda leaflet, countering accusations of Nationalist bombing atrocities with claims of Republican hypocrisy. The picture shows the church at Vinaroz being used as a CNT building.

THE BOMBARDMENT OF OPEN TOWNS

WHAT IS
A
MILITARY
OBJECTIVE?

IS THIS
A
MILITARY
OBJECTIVE?

THE CHURCH AT VINAROZ.
Vinaroz was taken by the Nationalists on April 15th, 1938.

The Spanish Government have turned this and other churches, which are always in "densely populated areas," into administrative headquarters and barracks.

Nationalists Reach Mediterranean

Left: Navarrese troops celebrating their arrival at Vinaroz on the Mediterranean coast, 15 April, which cut the Republican zone in two. An offensive against Valencia began a week later, commanded by General Aranda *(below, left)*, whose forces had taken Castellón, to the north of Valencia, by mid-June.

Right: Franco with his daughter Carmencita and her dog, called Dick.

Below: Listening secretly in the Republican zone to Mass broadcast by the Nationalists *(left)* and a re-instituted religious procession, guarded by armed peasants, in a village near Teruel recently taken by the Nationalists *(right)*.

Nationalist Air Power

Above: Italian planes on a bombing mission, from a documentary film about the Italian Legion Airforce in Spain.

Above left: English booklet attacking Italian military involvement in Spain.

Left: Dogfight on the Aragon front, by the Nationalist artist A. Kemer.

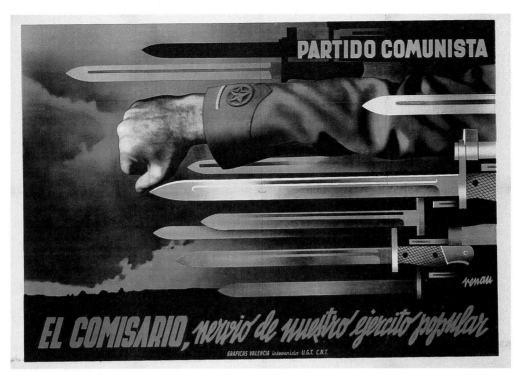

Posters to bolster the Republican forces:
Above: 'The commissar. Nerve of our Popular Army'; poster by Josep Renau promoting the role of the commissars, supported by the Communist Party.
Below left: A call for mechanics and skilled technicians to work for the Republican airforce.
Below right: Enlistment poster for the navy; the Republican fleet remained inactive for most of the war, suffering from low morale and a lack of experienced officers.

Republican troops crossing the River Ebro at Miravet, late July 1938.

9 · The Ebro Offensive

1938

July 5   Non-Intervention Committee approves plan to withdraw volunteers from Spain.

July 23   Nationalists within 20 miles of Valencia.

July 24   Popular Army launches Ebro offensive; battle of the River Ebro, greatest of the war, continues into November.

August 1   Nationalists contain Republican assault to south of Ebro.

August 10   Local Republican victories in Estremadura.

August 17   Negrín takes over Catalan munitions factories and reorganizes Cabinet after protest resignations of Basque and Catalan ministers.

August 18   Franco refuses all peace initiatives.

September 3   Nationalist armies break through at Gandesa on Ebro front.

September 16   Nationalists cross Ebro at Venta de Camposines.

September 29   Munich conference begins; resulting pact between Hitler, Mussolini, Chamberlain and Daladier ends Republic's hopes of Anglo-French help.

October 4   Foreign troops fighting for the Republic are withdrawn from line.

October 14   Several Italian units leave for home from Cádiz; more units follow over next month.

October 24   Trial of POUM leaders begins in Barcelona.

October 29   Farewell parade of International Brigades in Barcelona.

November 16   End of the battle of the Ebro; Popular Army retreats across river.

November 19   Franco agrees mining concessions to Germany.

November 29   Air attacks on Barcelona and Valencia.

Catalan cartoon of Franco pondering what to do on the Ebro front.

162

Republican posters encouraging the war industry:
Left: 'Make tanks. They are the vehicles of victory.' A poster by Martí Bas, member of the Spanish Communist Party and of the Union of Professional Artists that produced many of the war posters in Catalonia.
Above left: Notice of the first Congress of UGT Catalonian Metalworkers, promoting 'a powerful war industry', September 1938.
Above right: 'Comrades. Show your anti-Fascist spirit by working intensively'; an appeal by the union of gas, water, electricity and allied industries in the Levante.
Below: Workers in a munitions factory in Barcelona.

Battle of the Ebro, July-November 1938

The last major Republican offensive, planned by General Rojo to divert the Nationalist forces, began successfully on 24/25 July. The Republican troops reached Gandesa but fierce Nationalist counter-attacks changed success into a terrible war of attrition. By 18 November the Republican forces had retreated, with heavy losses of men, planes and weapons.

Above: Timber yard in Barcelona producing boats for the Ebro crossing.
Below: Crossing the Ebro by boat on 25 July *(left)* and casualties in the hospital train behind the lines *(right)*.

Above left: General Rojo, strategic brain of the Popular Army and planner of the Ebro offensive.
Above right: Republican infantry using one of the pontoon bridges erected after the initial boat crossing.
Below: Artillery action on the Ebro front: the Nationalists turned the battle into a major artillery contest.

Auxilio Social

EN NVESTRA JVSTICIA
ESTÁ NVESTRA FVERZA

C.S. de Tejada

Auxilio Social

The welfare organization of the Nationalists, Auxilio Social, had centres throughout the conquered territory and from 1937 was headed by Pilar Primo de Rivera, sister of the dead Falangist leader and founder of the Women's Falange. From October 1937 Franco's government required all women between the ages of 17 and 35 to undertake social work of some kind and continued to stress strictly traditional female roles.
Left: Poster for Auxilio Social by Carlos Sáenz de Tejada.
Below: Women handing out the white bread that was liberally distributed on the Nationalist take-over of new territory.
Right above: Gymnastics class for girls in the junior branch of the Women's Falange, Burgos, October 1938.
Right below: Posters of the Nationalist Youth Organizations aimed at girls: *(left)* for the festival of Epiphany, when Christmas presents are exchanged; *(right)* 'Today's girls and tomorrow's women united without class distinction.'

A través de la **O.J.** el **Regalo de los Reyes**

las niñas de hoy y las mujeres de mañana

UNIDAS SIN DISTINCION DE CLASES
EN ORGANIZACIONES JUVENILES DE F.E.T. Y DE LAS J.O.N-S.

Left: Franco with General Kindelán *(left),* commander of the Nationalist airforce, and General Vigon, his chief of staff, August 1938.

Above: One of the first Italian
units to leave for home from
Cádiz, in late autumn 1938.
Left: Motorcyclist dispatch rider at
Franco's Burgos headquarters,
August 1938.
Right above: Nationalist heavy
bomber of the Trechuelo squadron
on a raiding mission.
Right: Burning oil tanks in
Valencia after a Nationalist air
attack; Valencia came under
increased bombing at the end of
November.

¡EL SACRIFICIO DE LA VIDA ANTES QUE LA INVASION DE LA PATRIA!

PROPAGANDA Y PRENSA
SOCORRO ROJO DE ESPAÑA

GRAFICAS VALENCIA INTERVENIDO U.G.T. C.N.T.

War of Independence

As the war progressed, the Republic came to present it as a war of independence in which foreign invaders had to be repelled as the French had been in the Peninsular War of 1808-14.

Left: 'Sacrifice your life rather than allow the invasion of your country': a poster invoking the names of Daoiz and Velarde, heroes of 2 May 1808 in Madrid, and using one of Goya's famous prints of the horrors of the Peninsular War.

Below left: Catalan poster detailing foreign capitalist investors in Spain, 'the stranglers of the Spanish people and the real reason for the false neutrality'.

Below right; 'Spain's debt to the friends of the "Nationalists"'; a count of the Spanish ships sunk by German submarines during the First World War.

Right: 'Spain fights for its independence, for peace and solidarity among all peoples.'

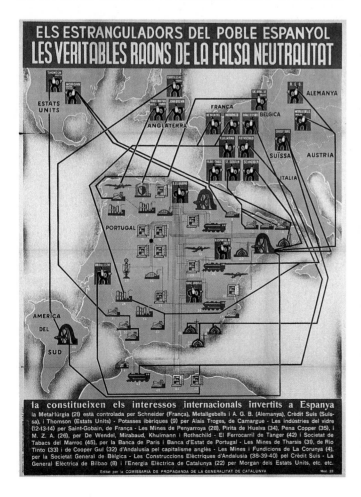

ESPAÑA LUCHA POR SU INDEPENDENCIA,
POR LA PAZ Y LA SOLIDARIDAD ENTRE TODOS LOS PUEBLOS

SUBSECRETARIA DE PROPAGANDA

171

Munich Pact

Left: Neville Chamberlain flanked by Hitler and the German Foreign Minister von Ribbentrop on his arrival at Munich for peace talks, 29 September 1938. The resulting pact between Daladier, Chamberlain, Mussolini and Hitler dashed hopes of any Anglo-French help for the Republic.
Left below: Prime Minister Negrín in Barcelona at the annual commemoration ceremony for the 1714 hero of Catalan independence, Rafael Casanovas, 11 September 1938.
Below: French Socialist poster appealing for funds to help Spanish and Czech refugees; under the Munich pact, much of Czechoslovakia had been ceded to Germany.

PEUPLE DE FRANCE
VERSE TON OBOLE POUR TES FRÈRES
D'ESPAGNE ET DE TCHÉCOSLOVAQUIE

Adressez les fonds au SECOURS SOCIALISTE S.F.I.O.
René JOUSSE, 12 cité Malesherbes, PARIS, 9ᵉ compte chèque postal Paris 2191-58
ou au Comité local

Departure of the International Brigades

Munich ended any possibility of a Russian/Anglo/French alliance against Hitler and in October 1938 Stalin agreed to the withdrawal of International Brigade members in Spain. Many of the survivors had already left, disillusioned or wounded or released on prisoner exchanges.

Above: British International Brigaders on their clearance from a Franco goal.

Above right: Flower-strewn leaving parade in Barcelona, 29 October 1938.

Right: Lincoln Brigade members aboard a French ship on their way home.

Below: Departure of wounded men and staff from the international hospital at Benicasím.

10 · Death of the Republic

1938

December 11 Republican plans dropped for sea-landing at Motril, Andalusia, together with offensive on Madrid front.

December 19 Germans take control of Montana and Tetuán mining operations.

December 23 Nationalist armies begin attack on Catalonia, smashing through Republican lines on Ebro/Segre front.

1939

January Nationalist armies sweep across Catalonia.

January 5 Popular Army attacks in Estremadura.

January 13 Tortosa falls to Nationalists.

January 15 Nationalists take Tarragona and Reus.

January 23 Republic declares martial law.

January 25 Negrín government abandons Barcelona; establishes headquarters at Figueras.

January 26 Barcelona falls to Navarrese, Moroccan and Italian troops; mass flight of refugees to French frontier.

January 31 Franco's troops enter Gerona; remaining Republican forces in Catalonia bombarded from air.

February 1 Cortes meets for the last time, at Castle of Figueras.

February 5 Azaña, Martínez Barrio, Companys and Aguirre leave Spain for France; thousands of refugees also cross Catalan border.

February 7 Negrín and General Rojo cross to France; General Miaja left in authority over remaining army.

February 8 Figueras taken by Nationalists.

February 9 Franco passes Law of Political Responsibilities, making anyone who had opposed the Nationalist movement guilty of crime.

February 10 Nationalists complete conquest of Catalonia. Negrín flies back from France to Alicante, in desperate attempt to prolong resistance after Franco's refusal to compromise.

February 16 Only General Miaja of army commanders supports Negrín's no-alternative policy of continued resistance.

February 27 President Azaña resigns over Negrín's policies; Martínez Barrio refuses presidency under the same conditions. Britain and France recognize Franco's government.

February 28 Nationalist planes bomb Republican strongholds in Valencia and Cartagena.

(continued on page 182)

Right: The Spanish Soldier, 'in memory of my friend who died in defence of Madrid'; Xavier Bueno, 1938.

Below: Refugee children leaving Barcelona for France, February 1939.

FALL OF CATALONIA

Exhausted, cold and half-starved, the Catalonians had lost the will to fight and Barcelona fell without a struggle to Franco's forces on 26 January; half a million refugees fled north to the French frontier.

Below: The port of Barcelona after aerial bombardment, early 1939.
Bottom: Prisoners rounded up in the Montjuich Citadel, Barcelona, 8 February.
Right above: Republican prisoner meeting up by chance with his brother, fighting with Franco's forces, in Tarragona, January 1939.
Far right: Women making the Fascist salute from a balcony in the Paseo de Gracía *(above)* during the procession of Nationalist troops through Barcelona *(below)*.
Right below: The first public mass in Barcelona since the start of the war, celebrated in the Plaza de Cataluña, 27 January.

Above: Exodus; painting by Aurelio Arteta.
Below: Wounded men reaching the French frontier.
Right above: The Road to France, 7 February 1939; painting by Jesús Martí.
Right below: Refugees making their way north after the fall of Catalonia.

Left above: Franco as Admiral of the Spanish Nationalist Fleet reviewing naval forces aboard the cruiser *Canarias* at Tarragona; part of the victory celebrations after the fall of Barcelona.

Left centre: Condor Legion officers planning the final offensive in an operations room at Lérida.

Left below: Navarrese troops with their monarchist flag reaching the French/Spanish village of Perthus, February 1939; their arrival sealed the frontier to later refugees.

Below: Prison cells established by the Communist military interrogation organization, SIM, in the Convent of Vallmajor, Barcelona; revealed after the Nationalist take-over of the city.

Right above: Spanish refugee children, dressed in Russian sailor suits, arriving to welcome in Moscow; Russia accepted about 5000 children and 2000 Communists from Spain during the course of the war, small numbers compared with other countries, particularly France.

Right below: Republican prisoners constructing a bridge in Palma, Majorca, February 1939; the island had been an Italian naval and air base since early in the war.

(continued from page 174)

1939

March 2　Negrín changes military commands, deposing Miaja and promoting Communist officers in charge of Alicante and Cartagena.

March 4-6　Confused military revolt against Negrín at Cartagena; attempts to take over naval base fail.

March 5　Anti-Negrín Council of National Defence set up in Madrid, initiated by Colonel Casado and presided over by Socialist Besteiro.

March 6　Negrín flees to Dakar; temporary seat of government at Elda deserted by 7th.

March 7-12　Fierce street fighting in Madrid between Communists and Casado's Defence Council supporters, including CNT militia units. Nationalist attack on Madrid in midst of chaos fails.

March 15　Hitler marches into Prague.

March 24-26　Casado attempts unsuccessfully to negotiate peace terms with Franco at Burgos.

March 26　Franco's final offensive.

March 27　Nationalist troops enter Madrid. Burgos regime joins Anti-Comintern Pact.

March 28　Mass flight from Madrid.

March 29　Franco's troops occupy Cuenca, Ciudad Real, Jaén and Albacete.

March 30　Valencia and Alicante taken; refugees try to escape from Alicante port.

March 31　Cartagena and last Republican strongpoints capitulate.

April 1　Franco announces end of war. US recognizes Franco's government.

Full-scale repression follows. Spain maintains a neutrality favourable to the Axis powers in World War II; in 1945 United Nations declares 'Fascist' Spain unfit for membership, but in 1953 USA signs a defence agreement with Franco. Franco regime continues till his death in 1975; in 1977 first democratic elections since 1936 are held.

Right: General Miaja arriving in Paris, March 1939; he was to die in exile.
Far right: Refugees making their way across the Pyrenees to France.

Above: The popular Socialist leader Julián Besteiro broadcasting the manifesto of the National Defence Council in Madrid, 5/6 March 1939; to his left is Colonel Casado, initiator of the Council in opposition to Negrín's policy of resistance.
Left: Madrid street during the fierce Republican feuding between Communists and supporters of the National Defence Council, 7-12 March.

FALL OF MADRID

After Casado's fruitless attempts to negotiate with Franco, Nationalist troops entered Madrid on 27 March; the shattered city was beyond resistance and surrendered without a fight.
Below: Nationalist troops overlooking Madrid, 1939.
Bottom right: Franco lunching at the front.
Bottom left: Bomb crater in a Madrid street.

Above: Moroccan troops squatting in the Plaza de la Villa, 28 March.
Right: Greeting the Nationalist victors in the Plaza de la Cebada.
Right below: Nuns arriving in the wake of the Nationalist troops to welcome from members of the Women's Falange.

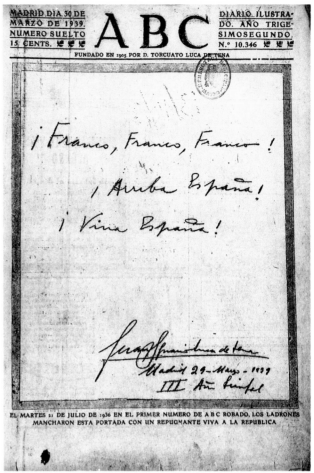

Above left: Nationalist poster published after the war: 'Financial aid for the fighter. I did my duty and so must you and everyone else.'

Above right: Cover of *ABC*, 30 March, proclaiming Franco's victory with the famous Nationalist slogan *'Viva España'*; the footnote deplores the 'repugnant *Viva a la Republica'* that appeared on the cover of 21 July 1936, the first issue of the paper after its take-over by 'thieves'.

Below: Franco at his desk, a framed picture of Hitler beside him.

Right: 'Spain resurrected'; published in Barcelona by the Nationalist Propaganda Department.

Victory Celebrations

Left: General Franco taking the salute at the march-past of Italian troops during the huge victory parade in Madrid, 19 May 1939.

Above left: Farewell march of the Condor Legion through the streets of León.

Above right: 'The glorious mutilated one', Millan Astray, founder of the Foreign Legion and close associate of Franco's, paying tribute to Portuguese troops during a leaving ceremony in Salamanca, 4 June 1939.

Below: Celebration dinner in Barcelona on the anniversary of the outbreak of war, 19 July 1939.

Top: Mural of Franco and his forces triumphant, in the Archivo Histórico Militar, Madrid.
Above: French internment camp at Bram, 1939. France was unable to cope with the huge influx of refugees and deaths were common in the overcrowded camps, where troops were penned behind barbed wire patrolled by guards and families were separated into camps for men and for women and children.

READING LIST

The following is a small selection from the many books published on the subject of the Spanish Civil War.

General history

Abella, Rafael *La vida cotidiana durante la guerra civil,* 2 vols (Barcelona, 1973, 1975)

Beevor, Antony *The Spanish Civil War* (London, 1982)

Bolloten, Burnett *The Spanish Revolution: The Left and the Struggle for Power* (London, 1979)

Brenan, Gerald *The Spanish Labyrinth* (Cambridge, 1943)

Carr, Raymond *Spain 1808-1939* (Oxford, 1966)

Carr, Raymond *The Spanish Tragedy: The Civil War in Perspective* (London, 1977)

Carr, Raymond, ed. *The Republic and the Civil War in Spain* (London, 1971)

Colodny, Robert *The Struggle for Madrid* (New York, 1958)

Jackson, Gabriel *The Spanish Republic and the Civil War 1931-1939* (Princeton, 1965)

Jackson, Gabriel *A Concise History of the Spanish Civil War* (New York, 1974)

Orwell, George *Homage to Catalonia* (London, 1938)

Payne, Stanley *Falange: A History of Spanish Fascism* (Stanford, 1961)

Payne, Stanley *The Spanish Revolution* (New York, 1970)

Preston, Paul *The Coming of the Spanish Civil War* (London, 1978)

Preston, Paul *War and Revolution in Spain 1931-34* (London, 1985)

Rojo, Vicente *España heroica* (Buenos Aires 1942)

Southworth, Herbert *Guernica! Guernica!* (California, 1977)

Thomas, Hugh *The Spanish Civil War* (3rd edition; London, 1977)

Trotsky, Leon *The Spanish Revolution, 1931-1939* (New York, 1973)

Tuñón, Manuel de Lara *et al La guerra civil española 50 años después* (Madrid, 1985)

International aspects

Brome, Vincent *The International Brigades, Spain 1936-1939* (London, 1965)

Casado, S. *The Last Days of Madrid* (London, 1939)

Castells, Andreu *Las brigadas internacionales de la guerra de España* (Barcelona, 1974)

Cattell, David *Communism and the Spanish Civil War* (Berkeley, 1955)

Cattell, David *Soviet Diplomacy and the Spanish Civil War* (Berkeley, 1957)

Edwards, Jill *The British Government & the Spanish Civil War, 1936-1939* (London, 1979)

Puzzo, Dante *Spain and the Great Powers, 1936-1941* (New York, 1962)

Watkins, K.W. *Britain Divided: The Effect of the Spanish Civil War on British Public Opinion* (London, 1963)

Weintraub, Stanley *The Last Great Cause: The Intellectuals and the Spanish Civil War* (London, 1968)

Fiction

Hemingway, Ernest *For Whom the Bell Tolls* (New York, 1940)

Lewis, Norman *The Day of the Fox* (London, 1957)

Malraux, André *L'Espoir* (Paris, 1938)

Sender, Ramón *Seven Red Sundays* (London, 1936)

Serge, Victor *The Case of Comrade Tulayev* (London, 1968); *Birth of Our Power* (London, 1968)

Spanish Civil War Verse (London, 1980)

Biography/Memoirs

Abad de Santillán, Diego *Memorias* (Barcelona, 1977)

Barea, Arturo *The Forging of a Rebel* (New York, 1946)

Fraser, Ronald *Blood of Spain: The Experience of Civil War 1936-1939* (London, 1979)

Gil Robles, José María *No fue posible la paz* (Barcelona, 1969)

Ibarruri, Dolores *They Shall Not Pass* (London, 1967; New York, 1976)

Langdon-Davies, John *Behind the Spanish Barricades* (New York, 1936)

Largo Caballero, F. *Mis recuerdos* (Mexico, 1956)

Maisky, Ivan *Spanish Notebooks* (London, 1966)

Romilly, Esmond *Boadilla* (London, 1971)

Steer, G.L. *The Tree of Gernika* (London, 1938)

PICTURE ACKNOWLEDGMENTS

The publishers would like to thank the following people for their help: Tony Atienza and Andrew Davies of the Marx Memorial Library, London; Susanna Tavera, photographer Richard Bristow and Ricardo Martí Morales, Barcelona; Antonio Gomez-Mendosa, Jesús Lozano, Gloria Luna, Col. Fernando Redondo of the Servicio Histórico Militar, Carlos Sáenz de Tejada, and Pilar Varela of the Hemeroteca Municipal, Madrid; Leland Stowe, Edward C. Weber and Maurice Levine in the USA; Roger Michaut and Conrad Caspari, Paris; Cristina Thompson of Allen and Unwin and the staff of Geoff Goode Photographics and Campaign Colour, London.

Photographs and illustrations were supplied by and are reproduced by kind permission of the following:

Abraham Lincoln Brigade Archives, Brandeis University, Boston: 17(B), 141(B), 148(B.r), 164(B.l); Alfonso, Madrid: 29(T), 33(T), 37(B), 40(T), 50(B), 51, 83(T,r), 102-3, 108(B), 157(B.l), 182-3; Amicale des Anciens Volontaires Français en Espagne Républicaine: 91(T); Archivo General de la Administración Civil del Estado, Alcalá de Henares, Madrid: 27(B), 33(B), 42; Archivo Histórico Nacional, Salamanca: 115; Archivo Inconográfico, Barcelona: 83(T,l), 114, 178(T); José Mario Armero, Madrid: 106(T), 107(B); Associated Press, London: 32(T), 49(T), 61(T), 184(B,l); Bridgeman Art Library, London: 119; Camera Press, London: 117(B,l); Agustí Centelles, Barcelona: 15(T), 36(T&B), 53(all), 56(T&B), 57(all), 64(B), 65(T,r&B), 69, 78(B,l), 88, 90(T), 123(B), 124(B,l&r), 125(T), 136(T), 140, 148(T&B,l), 153(T), 154(B), 190(B,l&r); Centro Internacional de la Historia, Barcelona: 11(B), 15(B), 47(T), 54(T), 78(B,r), 79, 86, 94, 95(T&B), 111 (T,r&B,r), 131, 134(B,l&r), 135, 140(T&B), 141(T,l), 142, 143(B,l,c&r), 151(T,l&r), 159(all), 163(T,l), 170(T&B,l&r), 171; Annabel Davies Collection, London: 1, 8(T), 13(B), 22(T), 26(T), 26(B,l), 28, 29(B), 30, 32(B,l&r), 34(inset), 35(B,r), 40(B), 41(T,l), 42, 43(T,l), 44(T,l), 52, 55(B; Branguli, Barcelona), 60(B), 82, 90(C), 98(B,l), 100(T&B), 109(B), 111(B,l) 120-21(all), 124(T,l&r), 136(B,r), 146-7, 179(B); René Dazy, Paris: 81(B,l), 87(B), 91(B,r), 97(B,r); Edimedia: 25, 91(B,r), 172(B,r), 175, 182(B,r); Efe, Madrid: endpapers, 8-9(B), 17(T), 24, 41(B), 43(T,r&C), 44(B), 45(T&B), 48(T), 49(B), 85(T,l), 89(B,r), 96(T), 104(T), 111(T,l), 128(T&B), 129(T), 138(C), 139(T), 141(T,r), 149(C), 156(T), 165(B), 168(B), 174, 176-7, 177(all), 180(B.r), 181(B), 185(all), 189(T,r); Fundación Figueras, Barcelona: 11(T), 26(T), 34, 35(T&B,l), 54(B), 62, 63(T), 66, 67, 99, 110, 134(T), 162, 163(T,r), 166(T), 167(B,l&r), 186(T,l), 187; Hemeroteca Municipal, Madrid: 10(T), 40(T&B), 76(T,r), 109(T,l), 125(B,l&r), 186(T,r); John Hillelson Agency Ltd, London: 60(T), 188(B,l); Illustrated London News: 89(T); Imperial War Museum, London: 105(B,l&R), 132(T&B), 165(T,l&r), 173(T,l); Institut de Fotografics de Catalunya, Barcelona (photo Merletti): 163(B), 189(B); Instituto Municipal de Historia, Barcelona: 12-13(B), 48(B,l), 52, 69(B), 78(T), 85(B), 87(T), 89(B,l), 97(C), 122-23, 152(T); Keystone Press, Paris: 16, 41(T,r), 50(T), 55(T), 64(T), 72(all), 73, 76(T,l), 97(T&B,l), 104(C&B,r); Jesús Lozano, Madrid: 31(B), 43(B), 48(B,r), 65(C), 81(B,r), 84(all), 91(B,l), 101(T&B), 106(B), 108(T), 117(B,r), 125(B,c), 132(inset), 145(T), 149(T,r), 156(B,l), 160-61, 166(B), 167(T), 168(T,l), 172(B,l); Ricardo Martí Morales: 151(C,r); Marx Memorial Library, London: 18(T&B), 20(T), 20-21, 44(C), 80, 90(B,l), 92(T,l&r&B), 93(all), 96(B), 105(T), 107(T,l), 109(T,r), 129(B), 130, 133(all), 136(B,l), 137, 138-39, 143(T), 144(C&B,l&r), 149(B), 152(B,l&r), 156(B,r), 158(T,r), 164(T&B,l) 173(T,r&B), 178(B); Oroñoz, Madrid: 151(B), 190(T), 192; Vasquez Parlade: 23(T); Photosource, London: 70(T&B), 92(C), 98(T), 105(T), 144(T), 154-55, 168-69, 173(C,r), 176(B), 180(B,l), 183(B); Popperfoto, London: 31(T), 37(T), 61(B), 68(T), 104(B,l), 107(T,r), 145(B), 172(T), 181(T), 184(B,r); Carlos Sáenz de Tejada, Madrid: 14, 46, 77, 126, 127; Salmer, Barcelona: 27(T), 40, 179(T); Servicio Histórico Militar, Madrid: 63(B), 65(T,l), 68(C&B,l&r), 74(B), 75(T), 83(C), 112(all), 113(T&B), 116(T), 117(T), 150, 153(B), 155(B), 158(B); Ullstein Bilderdienst, Berlin: 74(T), 116(T), 180(C,l), 184(T), 186(B), 189(T,l); University of Michigan, Labadie Collection: 22(B), 90(B,r), 118(B,r), 123(T).